A Guide to Estate Wills, Conflicts, and Resolutions

C. P. Kumar
Reiki Healer
Roorkee - 247667, India

Disclaimer

While every effort has been made to ensure the accuracy and completeness of the content in this book, the author cannot guarantee that the information contained herein is error-free, up-to-date, or suitable for every individual circumstance.

The author shall not be held liable or responsible for any errors or omissions in the content of the book, nor for any damages, or losses that may arise from any actions taken based upon the suggestions or contents presented in the book.

Readers are advised to use their own judgment and discretion in applying the information provided in this book, and to consult with qualified professionals before taking any action based on the contents of this book. The author disclaims any and all liability or responsibility for any actions taken or not taken based on the information contained in this book.

DEDICATION

To all those who seek to secure their legacy, protect their loved ones, and navigate the intricate path of estate planning with wisdom and foresight.

In the journey of life, we often accumulate not just wealth but also cherished memories, enduring bonds, and a profound desire to provide for those we hold dear. Crafting a will is an essential part of that journey, a testament to our love and responsibility toward the future.

This book, "A Guide to Estate Wills, Conflicts, and Resolutions", is dedicated to you - the individuals, families, and professionals who recognize the importance of meticulous planning, the significance of clear communication, and the value of resolution over discord.

Within these pages, we explore the intricacies of estate planning, from the legal formalities that underpin your will's validity to the complexities of managing diverse assets. We delve into the financial costs, tax implications, and the ever-evolving landscape of life circumstances that can shape your estate plan.

We address the profound decisions, such as selecting guardians for your precious ones and the emotional complexities of disinheriting heirs. You will gain insights into the pivotal role of executors, the probate process, and the potential conflicts that may arise among beneficiaries.

But this book isn't just about conflicts; it's about solutions. We shed light on mediation and alternative dispute resolution methods, showcasing a path to harmony even in the face of disagreement. Through it all, we underscore the paramount importance of clear communication and the guidance of professionals in crafting a will that stands the test of time.

As you embark on your journey through these chapters, may you find the knowledge, insight, and inspiration needed to safeguard your legacy, uphold your values, and nurture the bonds that make your family unique. May your will not only be a legal document but a reflection of your enduring love and care.

This dedication is a tribute to your commitment to securing a brighter future, one where conflicts are minimized, and the legacy you leave behind is a testament to your wisdom and compassion.

With heartfelt dedication,

C. P. Kumar
Reiki Healer
Former Scientist 'G', National Institute of Hydrology
Roorkee - 247667, India
E-mail: cpkumar@yahoo.com
Web: https://www.angelfire.com/nh/cpkumar/virgo.html

CONTENTS

Copyright 2

Disclaimer 3

DEDICATION..4

PREFACE 8

Chapter 1.   Introduction to Estate Planning 9

Chapter 2.   Legal Requirements for Wills...........................15

Chapter 3.   Complex Estate Assets....................................21

Chapter 4.   Financial Costs of Estate Planning 26

Chapter 5.   Estate Taxes 33

Chapter 6.   Changing Life Circumstances...........................39

Chapter 7.   Guardianship for Minors..................................46

Chapter 8.   Disinheriting Heirs...52

Chapter 9.   Executor Selection and Responsibilities.............58

Chapter 10.   Probate Process..65

Chapter 11.   Conflict Resolution Among Beneficiaries..........71

Chapter 12.   Challenges to Disinheritance............................77

Chapter 13.   Mediation in Estate Disputes...........................83

Chapter 14.   Litigation and Its Consequences........................88

Chapter 15.   Alternative Dispute Resolution (ADR) Methods
....94

Chapter 16.   The Importance of Clear Communication........101

Chapter 17.   Professional Guidance in Estate Planning........108

PREFACE

Estate planning is a vital but often complex undertaking. In "A Guide to Estate Wills, Conflicts, and Resolutions", we will navigate this intricate terrain together. This book is your compass, guiding you through the multifaceted world of estate planning.

We start by highlighting the importance of estate planning and the legal requirements for creating a valid will. As we delve into the complexities of managing diverse assets and the associated financial costs, you will gain a comprehensive understanding of the process.

Estate taxes and the impact of changing life circumstances are explored, emphasizing the need to keep your will current. Decisions regarding guardianship for minors and disinheritance come under scrutiny, along with the critical role of executors and the probate process.

We then delve into the potential conflicts that may arise among beneficiaries, addressing challenges to disinheritance and discussing dispute resolution options, including mediation and alternative methods.

Throughout this journey, we stress the importance of clear communication and seeking professional guidance from legal and financial experts.

Your journey into the world of estate planning, conflicts, and resolutions begins here. This book serves as your trusted guide, helping you protect your legacy and the well-being of your loved ones.

C. P. Kumar

Introduction

Estate planning is a critical aspect of financial management that often goes overlooked until it's too late. Many individuals mistakenly believe that estate planning is only for the wealthy, but in reality, it is a process that can benefit people from all walks of life. In this comprehensive guide to estate planning, we will delve into the fundamental principles and importance of creating a will as a crucial part of this process. Understanding the significance of estate planning and the role of wills can help you make informed decisions that secure your legacy and protect your loved ones.

The Essence of Estate Planning

Estate planning is the strategic and systematic process of managing your assets, finances, and affairs during your lifetime and distributing them after your death according to your wishes. It involves a series of legal and financial strategies that aim to maximize the value of your estate while minimizing taxes and administrative costs. Estate planning is not just about wealth transfer; it encompasses a wide range of considerations, including healthcare decisions, guardianship of minor children, and charitable giving.

One of the fundamental goals of estate planning is to ensure that your assets are distributed according to your wishes, rather than being subject to intestacy laws, which vary from one jurisdiction to another. Effective estate planning can help you:

- Provide financial security for your family and dependents
- Minimize estate taxes and other financial burdens
- Appoint guardians for minor children
- Plan for incapacity and medical decisions
- Support charitable causes close to your heart
- Avoid family conflicts and legal disputes

The Importance of a Will

A will is a cornerstone of estate planning. It is a legal document that outlines your instructions for the distribution of your assets, the care of your dependents, and the appointment of an executor who will oversee the fulfillment of your wishes. Here's why creating a will is a crucial part of estate planning.

1. Asset Distribution

A will allows you to specify how your assets should be distributed upon your death. Without a will, your estate may be distributed according to state laws, which may not align with your intentions. This can result in assets going to unintended beneficiaries or loved ones being left without the support they need.

Your will can address various assets, including real estate, personal property, investments, and sentimental items. You can make specific bequests to individuals or organizations, ensuring that your wishes are honored.

2. Guardianship for Minor Children

If you have minor children, a will is where you can appoint a guardian to care for them in the event of your death. This is a crucial decision that should not be left to chance or contentious legal battles. By naming a guardian in your will, you provide clarity and peace of mind for your children's future.

3. Executor Appointment

In your will, you can designate an executor, also known as a personal representative or administrator. The executor is responsible for carrying out the instructions in your will, including settling debts, paying taxes, and distributing assets. Appointing a competent executor ensures that your wishes are faithfully executed.

4. Avoiding Intestacy Laws

Dying without a will means dying intestate. In such cases, state laws dictate how your assets are distributed. The results may not align with your preferences and can lead to unnecessary legal complications and family disputes. A well-crafted will gives you control over the distribution of your estate.

5. Minimizing Estate Taxes

Estate taxes can substantially diminish the value of your estate, leaving less for your beneficiaries. Through careful estate planning and the use of various strategies, you can minimize estate taxes and preserve more of your wealth for your loved ones. A will can include provisions that help reduce tax liabilities.

The Will as a Living Document

It's important to note that a will is not a static document. Life circumstances change, and your will should reflect these changes to remain effective. Regular reviews of your will are essential, especially when significant life events occur, such as marriage, divorce, the birth of children, or the acquisition of new assets.

Updating your will ensures that it accurately reflects your current wishes and circumstances. Failing to do so can lead to unintended consequences and legal challenges.

Professional Guidance in Estate Planning

While it's possible to create a basic will using online templates or do-it-yourself kits, estate planning is a complex and highly individualized process. Engaging the services of a qualified estate planning attorney is strongly recommended. An attorney can help you navigate the intricate legal and financial aspects of estate planning, ensuring that your plan is tailored to your unique needs and goals.

When seeking professional guidance in estate planning, consider the following:

1. Attorney Expertise

Estate planning attorneys specialize in the intricacies of estate law. They can provide valuable insights, identify potential pitfalls, and help you make informed decisions.

2. Personalized Solutions

An attorney can customize your estate plan to address your specific objectives and concerns, ensuring that it aligns with your values and goals.

3. Legal Compliance

Estate planning involves adherence to state and federal laws. A knowledgeable attorney will ensure that your plan complies with all relevant legal requirements.

4. Minimizing Taxation

Estate planning attorneys are well-versed in tax laws and can help you employ strategies to minimize estate taxes and maximize the inheritance your beneficiaries receive.

5. Reducing Family Conflicts

Professional guidance can help reduce the likelihood of disputes among family members by ensuring that your intentions are clearly and legally documented.

Conclusion

Estate planning is an essential financial and legal process that everyone should undertake regardless of their wealth or age. Central to this process is the creation of a will, a legal document that outlines your wishes for asset distribution, guardianship of minor children, and executorship. A well-structured estate plan, including a will, provides you with control over your legacy, minimizes the burden of taxes and administrative costs, and ensures that your loved ones are taken care of according to your desires.

Estate planning is not a one-time endeavor; it is a dynamic process that should evolve with your changing circumstances. Regular reviews and updates to your will are crucial to maintaining its relevance and effectiveness.

Seeking the expertise of an estate planning attorney is a prudent step in creating a comprehensive and legally sound estate plan. With professional guidance, you can navigate the complexities of estate law, minimize potential conflicts, and secure a brighter financial future for yourself and your loved ones.

Introduction

In the intricate world of estate planning and the distribution of assets after one's demise, the importance of a well-structured and legally sound will cannot be overstated. A will, often referred to as a last will and testament, serves as a critical document to ensure that your wishes regarding your estate are carried out as you desire. However, for a will to be legally valid, it must adhere to specific legal requirements and formalities. In this article, we will delve into the legal requirements for wills, providing you with a comprehensive understanding of the fundamental elements necessary to create a valid will.

Testamentary Capacity

One of the foundational legal requirements for a valid will is the testamentary capacity of the testator. A testator is a person who creates a legally valid will to specify the distribution of their assets upon their death. Testamentary capacity refers to the mental and cognitive ability of the person creating the will to understand the implications and consequences of their actions. The testator must be of sound mind, which typically means that they should:

Understand the nature and extent of their property: The testator must have a reasonable understanding of their assets, including real estate, financial holdings, and personal belongings.

Recognize their immediate family and potential beneficiaries: The testator should be able to identify their close family members and intended beneficiaries, as well as understand the implications of their choices.

Comprehend the purpose and effect of the will: It is essential that the testator understands that they are creating a document that will dictate how their assets will be distributed upon their death.

Not be subject to undue influence or coercion: The testator's decisions must be made freely and without any external pressure or manipulation.

Ensuring testamentary capacity is a crucial step in avoiding potential challenges to the validity of the will in the future.

Age Requirement

Another fundamental legal requirement for creating a valid will is that the testator must be of a certain age, typically referred to as the "age of majority." In most jurisdictions, this age is set at 18 years old. Minors are generally not considered legally competent to make a will. However, there may be exceptions, such as emancipated minors, who may have the capacity to create a valid will. Emancipated minors are individuals under the age of 18 who have been granted legal independence from their parents or guardians, typically due to demonstrating the ability to support themselves and make responsible decisions.

Voluntary and Willful Execution

The creation of a will must be a voluntary and willful act on the part of the testator. This means that the testator should not be under any duress, undue influence, or coercion when making their will. They should be making decisions regarding the distribution of their estate of their own accord, free from external pressures.

Writing Requirement

A will must typically be in writing to be considered legally valid. Although some jurisdictions allow oral wills (known as nuncupative wills) in specific circumstances, they are generally subject to strict limitations and are not recognized in many places. To ensure the validity of your will, it is advisable to put it in writing.

Signature of the Testator

One of the most critical legal formalities for a will is the signature of the testator. The testator must sign the will personally at the end of the document. The signature is a clear indication of the testator's intent and verifies that the document indeed represents their final wishes.

In some cases, if the testator is unable to sign due to physical limitations, they may be allowed to make a mark or have someone sign on their behalf in their presence and at their direction. This is typically referred to as a "proxy signature" and may require additional witnesses or notary acknowledgment to validate.

Witness Signatures

Most jurisdictions require wills to be witnessed by one or more individuals who are not beneficiaries under the will. These witnesses play a critical role in confirming the authenticity and voluntariness of the testator's signature. The witnesses must be of legal age and possess the mental capacity to understand the significance of their role as witnesses.

The witnessing process typically involves the following steps:

1. The testator signs the will in the presence of the witnesses.

2. The witnesses then sign the will in the presence of the testator and each other.

3. Some jurisdictions may require that the witnesses sign affidavits affirming that they observed the testator signing the will and that they believe the testator was of sound mind and not under duress.

Witnesses serve as impartial verifiers, helping to prevent fraud and confirming that the will was executed in accordance with the law.

Notarization

Notarization is the process of having a notary public verify the authenticity of signatures on documents and ensure their legal validity by affixing an official seal or stamp. While notarization is not always a strict legal requirement for wills, it can be a valuable step in the process. Having a will notarized involves having a notary public certify the authenticity of the testator's signature and the witnesses' signatures. Notarization adds an extra layer of protection against potential challenges to the will's validity.

Revocation and Amendment

As life circumstances change, individuals may need to amend or revoke their existing wills. To ensure that these changes are legally effective, it is essential to follow specific legal requirements.

Revocation of a will: A testator can revoke their will in various ways, including physically destroying the document, creating a new will with explicit language revoking the old one, or executing a formal revocation document in accordance with local laws.

Codicils: Codicils are legal documents used to make amendments or additions to an existing last will and testament, typically used to modify specific provisions without creating an entirely new will. Instead of creating an entirely new will, a testator may choose to make minor amendments or additions to their existing will using a codicil. A codicil is a legal document that must be executed with the same formalities as a will.

Holographic Wills

In some jurisdictions, holographic wills are recognized as valid under certain conditions. A holographic will is a will entirely written, dated, and signed by the testator in their handwriting, often without the need for witnesses. However, not all states or countries accept holographic wills, so it is crucial to consult local laws to determine their validity.

Legal Advice and Professional Guidance

Creating a legally valid will can be a complex process, and it is advisable to seek legal advice and professional guidance when doing so. Estate planning attorneys are well-versed in the legal requirements for wills and can help ensure that your will complies with local laws and accurately reflects your wishes.

Conclusion

A well-drafted and legally valid will is a cornerstone of effective estate planning. Understanding the legal requirements for wills is essential to ensure that your final wishes are carried out as intended and that your estate is distributed according to your preferences. By adhering to the fundamental legal formalities outlined in this article, you can help protect the validity of your will and provide peace of mind for both yourself and your loved ones. However, because laws regarding wills can vary significantly by jurisdiction, it is always advisable to consult with a qualified legal professional to navigate the complexities of estate planning and will creation effectively.

Introduction

Estate planning is a vital process that ensures your assets are distributed according to your wishes after your passing. Yet, for many, estate planning is not a straightforward task. Complex estate assets, comprised of diverse holdings, investments, and properties, can create significant challenges in the process of creating a comprehensive will. In this article, we will delve into the intricacies of complex estate assets, examining the challenges they present and offering insights into how to navigate them effectively. Understanding these complexities is essential for anyone embarking on the journey of estate planning, as it can greatly impact the successful resolution of your estate.

The Multifaceted Nature of Complex Estate Assets

Estate assets can range from simple bank accounts and real estate to intricate investments, businesses, intellectual property, and sentimental items. When these various components intertwine, they form what we refer to as complex estate assets. The primary challenge of managing diverse assets within your will lies in recognizing their unique characteristics, values, and implications.

1. Valuation Challenges

One of the foremost complexities of managing diverse estate assets is determining their value accurately. Different assets have distinct valuation methodologies, and their values may fluctuate over time. For instance, while assessing the value of a bank account is relatively straightforward, valuing a family business or intellectual property rights can be highly intricate. Failure to assess asset values accurately can lead to uneven distribution, tax consequences, and potential conflicts among beneficiaries.

2. Tax Implications

Estate taxes and inheritance taxes can have a significant impact on the distribution of complex assets. Each jurisdiction has its tax laws and regulations, and they often treat various assets differently. Assets such as retirement accounts, real estate, and investments may be subject to different tax rates and exemptions. Understanding the tax implications of each asset is crucial to minimizing the tax burden on your heirs and ensuring the efficient transfer of wealth.

3. Asset Liquidity

Some complex assets, such as real estate or closely held businesses, may lack liquidity. Liquidity refers to an asset's ability to be quickly converted into cash without significantly impacting its market value. When complex assets lack liquidity, it can create challenges for beneficiaries who may require immediate access to funds for various purposes, including settling debts or covering estate-related expenses.

4. Family Dynamics

The presence of diverse assets can exacerbate existing family dynamics and potential conflicts among heirs. A valuable family business, for example, can lead to disputes among siblings or other family members who have differing visions for its future. Addressing these dynamics within your will is essential to prevent prolonged legal battles and maintain family harmony.

Strategies for Navigating Complex Estate Assets

While managing complex estate assets can be challenging, there are several strategies that can help streamline the process and reduce the risk of conflicts and complications.

1. Comprehensive Documentation

Thorough and accurate documentation is the foundation of effective estate planning. Create a detailed inventory of all your assets, including their location, value, and ownership structure. This inventory should encompass financial accounts, real estate holdings, investment portfolios, business interests, and any intellectual property or valuable personal items.

2. Professional Guidance

Seeking the assistance of experienced professionals, such as estate attorneys, financial advisors, and accountants, is invaluable when dealing with complex estate assets. These experts can provide guidance on tax planning, asset valuation, and the legal intricacies of your estate. They can also help you navigate the unique challenges posed by your specific assets.

3. Asset Allocation and Distribution

Consider the desires and financial needs of your beneficiaries when allocating and distributing assets. For example, if you have one heir interested in running a family business and another who prefers cash, create a plan that accommodates both preferences. This may involve setting up trusts or establishing specific conditions for asset distribution.

4. Regular Updates

Estate planning is not a one-time task. As the value and nature of your assets change over time, it's essential to revisit and update your estate plan accordingly. This includes reviewing beneficiary designations, updating wills and trusts, and adjusting asset allocation strategies.

5. Open Communication

Encourage open and honest communication with your heirs about your estate plans. Discussing your intentions and the reasons behind your decisions can help prevent misunderstandings and conflicts in the future. It also provides an opportunity for heirs to ask questions and seek clarification.

6. Consideration of Business Succession

If you own a business, developing a clear business succession plan is paramount. This plan outlines how the business will be transferred or managed after your passing. It can involve selecting a successor, setting up a buy-sell agreement, or establishing a trust to ensure the continuity of the business.

7. Charitable Giving

For individuals with a philanthropic inclination, charitable giving can be an effective strategy for managing complex estate assets. Donating assets to charitable organizations or establishing charitable trusts can provide tax benefits and leave a lasting legacy.

Conclusion

Complex estate assets can present numerous challenges in the estate planning process. Valuation discrepancies, tax implications, liquidity concerns, family dynamics, and the diversity of assets themselves can complicate the distribution of your wealth. However, with careful consideration, comprehensive documentation, and the guidance of experienced professionals, you can navigate these complexities effectively and ensure a smooth transition of your assets to your chosen beneficiaries.

Remember that estate planning is not a static endeavor. Regular updates and open communication with your heirs are essential to adapt to changing circumstances and prevent conflicts. By addressing the unique complexities of your estate assets head-on, you can create a will that reflects your intentions and provides financial security for your loved ones, ultimately leading to the successful resolution of your estate.

In the end, estate planning is not just about managing wealth; it's about leaving a lasting legacy and ensuring that your assets benefit your family and the causes you care about long after you're gone.

Introduction

Estate planning is a crucial aspect of an individual's financial journey, aimed at ensuring the smooth transition of assets to heirs and beneficiaries upon one's passing. While many view estate planning as a means to secure their family's financial future, it is essential to understand that it comes with its own set of financial costs. In this article, we will explore the financial costs of estate planning, focusing primarily on the legal fees and associated expenses that individuals may incur when creating, updating, and administering a will.

The Importance of Estate Planning

Before delving into the financial aspects of estate planning, it is imperative to establish the significance of this process. Estate planning is not just reserved for the wealthy; it is a fundamental responsibility for anyone who wishes to protect their assets, ensure their wishes are followed, and reduce the burden on their loved ones during a difficult time.

1. Asset Protection

Estate planning allows individuals to protect their assets from unnecessary taxes, creditors, and legal disputes. Proper planning can minimize the erosion of an estate's value, ensuring that more wealth is passed on to beneficiaries.

2. Wishes and Instructions

A well-structured estate plan, including a will, ensures that your wishes are explicitly stated and legally binding. It helps prevent conflicts among family members and provides clarity regarding asset distribution.

3. Guardianship for Minors

Estate planning allows parents to designate guardians for their minor children, ensuring their care and upbringing according to the parents' preferences in case of unexpected events.

4. Healthcare Decisions

Estate planning also includes documents like a healthcare proxy and living will, which provide instructions on medical decisions in case of incapacitation. This ensures that your healthcare choices are respected.

Creating a Will: Legal Fees and Costs

1. Attorney Fees

One of the primary expenses associated with estate planning is hiring an attorney to help create a will. The complexity of your estate, the specific provisions you require, and the attorney's expertise will all impact the cost. On average, attorney fees for drafting a will can range from a few hundred to several thousand dollars.

2. Legal Consultations

Before drafting a will, it is advisable to consult with an attorney to discuss your specific circumstances and goals.

While this consultation may not be as costly as drafting the entire will, it still adds to the overall expense of estate planning.

3. Executor Compensation

It is common to appoint an executor in your will to oversee the distribution of assets and ensure your wishes are carried out. In many cases, executors are entitled to compensation, which is typically a percentage of the estate's value. This can add to the overall cost of administering the will.

4. Notary and Witness Fees

Most jurisdictions require wills to be notarized and witnessed to be valid. The fees associated with notary services and witnesses can vary but are an additional expense to consider when creating a will.

Updating an Existing Will

Estate planning is not a one-and-done process; it requires periodic updates to reflect changes in your life, assets, and wishes. Here are some financial considerations when updating an existing will:

1. Attorney Fees for Revisions

If you need to make changes to your will, whether due to changes in beneficiaries, assets, or other factors, you will likely need to pay attorney fees again. The cost will depend on the complexity of the revisions.

2. Codicils

In some cases, minor changes to a will can be made through a document called a codicil, which is an amendment to the existing will. Codicils may be a more cost-effective option compared to completely redrafting the will.

3. Regular Review

To minimize the financial impact of frequent revisions, it is advisable to regularly review your estate plan and make updates as needed. This can help you avoid major overhauls and their associated costs.

Administering a Will: Legal Fees and Costs

Once an individual passes away, their will enters the process of administration, which comes with its own set of financial costs.

1. Probate Fees

Probate is the legal process by which a will is validated and the assets of the deceased are distributed. Probate fees, also known as court fees, are typically calculated as a percentage of the estate's total value. The exact percentage varies by jurisdiction but can be substantial in larger estates.

2. Executor Fees

If an executor is named in the will, they are entitled to compensation for their services. Executor fees are usually set by state law and can be a percentage of the estate's value or a reasonable hourly rate.

3. Legal Fees for Probate

Legal representation may be required during the probate process, especially if disputes or complex issues arise. These legal fees are often paid from the estate's assets, further reducing the assets available for distribution to beneficiaries.

4. Accountant Fees

In some cases, an accountant may be hired to handle financial matters related to the estate, such as preparing tax returns. Their fees are also typically paid from the estate.

Strategies to Minimize Estate Planning Costs

While estate planning inevitably involves costs, there are strategies to minimize these financial burdens.

1. DIY Will Kits

DIY (do-it-yourself) Will Kits are pre-made tools that individuals can use to create their own last will and testament without the help of an attorney, but legal consultation is often recommended to ensure compliance with local laws. For individuals with straightforward estates and simple wishes, do-it-yourself (DIY) will kits are an affordable option. However, caution is advised, as mistakes or omissions in a self-created will can lead to legal challenges.

2. Beneficiary Designations

Some assets, such as life insurance policies, retirement accounts, and bank accounts, allow you to designate beneficiaries directly. By keeping these designations up to date, you can bypass the probate process for these assets, reducing associated costs.

3. Trusts

Establishing trusts can be a more expensive upfront cost, but they can help avoid probate entirely for certain assets, ultimately saving money and time in the long run.

4. Regular Review and Communication

Regularly reviewing and communicating your estate plan with your attorney can help identify potential issues early on, reducing the need for major revisions and associated costs.

5. Fee Negotiation

It's essential to discuss fees and costs with your attorney upfront and, if possible, negotiate a fee structure that works for both parties. Some attorneys may offer flat fees for specific estate planning services.

6. Selecting the Right Attorney

Choose an attorney with expertise in estate planning to ensure that your plan is tailored to your needs, minimizing the risk of costly mistakes.

Conclusion

Estate planning is a critical financial endeavor that carries its own set of costs, primarily in the form of legal fees and associated expenses. While these expenses can vary widely based on individual circumstances and the complexity of the estate, they are an essential investment in securing the financial future of your loved ones and ensuring your wishes are carried out.

Understanding the financial costs of estate planning, from creating a will to administering an estate, is crucial for individuals looking to navigate this complex process. By being aware of these costs and exploring strategies to minimize them, you can achieve a more efficient and cost-effective estate plan that meets your goals and safeguards your assets for generations to come.

Introduction

Estate planning is a multifaceted endeavor that involves the careful consideration of various factors, from the distribution of assets to the resolution of conflicts among heirs and beneficiaries. Among these considerations, estate taxes occupy a central role. Understanding the implications of estate taxes on asset distribution and employing effective strategies to minimize tax liability is paramount for anyone seeking to preserve and pass on their wealth. In this article, we will delve into the world of estate taxes, exploring their impact on asset distribution and highlighting key strategies to minimize tax liability.

The Basics of Estate Taxes

Estate taxes, often referred to as inheritance taxes or death taxes, are levied on the transfer of an individual's estate upon their demise. These taxes are typically imposed on the net value of the estate, which includes various assets such as real estate, investments, bank accounts, personal property, and more. The rates and exemptions for estate taxes vary from one jurisdiction to another, and they can change over time due to legislative adjustments. Therefore, it is essential to stay informed about the specific regulations in your area.

Implications for Asset Distribution

1. Reduced Inheritance

One of the most immediate implications of estate taxes is a reduced inheritance for heirs and beneficiaries. The tax liability can significantly diminish the value of the estate that is ultimately passed on to loved ones. This reduction in inheritable assets can have a profound impact on the financial well-being of heirs, potentially altering their financial plans and aspirations.

2. Forced Asset Liquidation

In some cases, estate taxes may force heirs to sell certain assets to cover the tax bill. For instance, if a substantial portion of the estate consists of illiquid assets, such as real estate or closely-held businesses, heirs may find themselves in a challenging position. Liquidation of these assets may not only result in financial losses but also disrupt family legacies or business continuity.

3. Intra-Family Conflicts

Estate taxes can also be a source of intra-family conflicts. Disagreements may arise among heirs and beneficiaries over the allocation of tax liabilities and the distribution of remaining assets. These conflicts can lead to prolonged legal battles, emotional strain, and fractured family relationships.

Strategies to Minimize Tax Liability

Given the potential adverse effects of estate taxes, it is essential to employ effective strategies to minimize tax liability while still ensuring your assets are distributed according to your wishes. Here are some key strategies to consider:

1. Gifting Strategies

One effective way to reduce the taxable value of your estate is through gifting. You can gift assets to your heirs during your lifetime, thus lowering the overall estate value subject to taxation. There are annual and lifetime gift tax exclusions that allow you to gift a certain amount to each recipient without incurring gift taxes. However, it's crucial to be aware of these exclusions and their limitations, as exceeding them can trigger gift taxes.

2. Establishing Trusts

Trusts are powerful tools in estate planning that can help minimize tax liability. Irrevocable trusts, in particular, can remove assets from your estate for tax purposes, as you no longer have control over them once they are placed in the trust. Common types of irrevocable trusts include irrevocable life insurance trusts (ILITs), grantor-retained annuity trusts (GRATs), and charitable remainder trusts (CRTs). Each type of trust has its own specific benefits and considerations, so it's essential to consult with a qualified estate planning attorney to determine which trust(s) align with your goals.

An ILIT is a trust established to hold life insurance policies outside of the insured person's estate, providing potential estate tax benefits upon their death. A GRAT is an irrevocable trust where the grantor (who creates the trust) retains an annuity payment for a specific term, with any remaining assets passing to beneficiaries, often used as an estate planning tool to transfer wealth with reduced gift tax implications. A CRT is an irrevocable trust that provides income to beneficiaries for a set period, with the remaining assets eventually donated to a charitable organization, offering both income to beneficiaries and potential charitable tax deductions to the grantor (who establishes the trust and funds it).

3. Utilizing Spousal Portability

In many jurisdictions, estate tax laws allow for portability of the estate tax exemption between spouses. This means that if one spouse does not utilize their entire exemption, the unused portion can be transferred to the surviving spouse. Leveraging spousal portability can effectively double the available exemption amount for a married couple, providing significant tax savings.

4. Leveraging Life Insurance

Life insurance can serve as a valuable tool for offsetting estate taxes. By designating a life insurance policy to cover the anticipated tax liability, you can ensure that your heirs receive their intended inheritances without the burden of estate taxes. This strategy is particularly useful for individuals with substantial estates that may be subject to high tax rates.

5. Charitable Giving

Charitable giving can be a win-win strategy for reducing estate taxes while supporting causes that are important to you. Charitable bequests and contributions can be deducted from the taxable value of your estate. Establishing a charitable remainder trust (CRT) allows you to provide for your heirs while also benefiting a charitable organization, ultimately reducing the taxable value of your estate.

6. Business Succession Planning

For business owners, proper succession planning is critical to minimize estate tax liability. Strategies such as gifting shares to family members, implementing buy-sell agreements, or creating family limited partnerships (FLPs) can help transition business ownership to the next generation while minimizing tax exposure.

A Family Limited Partnership (FLP) is a legal structure that allows family members to pool their assets into a partnership, often for estate planning and wealth transfer purposes, while maintaining control over the assets through the general partner. The general partner is typically a family member or entity responsible for managing the partnership's assets and making decisions on behalf of the partnership. This general partner retains control over the assets and operations of the FLP, while limited partners (other family members) have limited influence and liability.

7. Keep Current with Tax Laws

Estate tax laws are subject to change, and staying informed about these changes is essential for effective estate planning. Periodically reviewing your estate plan with a qualified professional ensures that your strategies remain aligned with the current tax landscape and your financial goals.

Conclusion

Estate taxes are a significant consideration in the realm of estate planning, and their implications on asset distribution should not be underestimated. The reduction in inheritances, potential asset liquidation, and family conflicts that can arise from estate taxes underscore the importance of proactive tax minimization strategies. By incorporating techniques such as gifting, trusts, spousal portability, life insurance, charitable giving, and business succession planning, individuals can navigate the complex terrain of estate taxes with greater confidence and ensure that their wealth is preserved and distributed as they intend. As the tax landscape evolves, ongoing consultation with estate planning professionals remains essential to adapt strategies and safeguard the financial legacies we leave behind. In the end, a well-crafted estate plan not only minimizes tax liabilities but also fosters peace of mind for both the planner and their heirs.

Introduction

Estate planning is a responsible and essential task that allows individuals to ensure the orderly distribution of their assets and the welfare of their loved ones after they are gone. A well-crafted will is the cornerstone of any estate plan, offering peace of mind and clarity regarding one's wishes. However, life is unpredictable, and as circumstances change, so too should your will. In this article, we explore the ever-evolving nature of life events and family dynamics, highlighting the critical importance of regularly updating your will. We will navigate through various scenarios and discuss the significance of staying proactive in ensuring that your final wishes align with your current situation.

The Evolution of Life Events

Life is a dynamic journey filled with unforeseen twists and turns. Major life events can significantly impact your financial situation, relationships, and priorities. Here, we delve into some of these life events and how they may necessitate updates to your will.

1. Marriage and Partnership

Getting married or entering into a civil partnership is a joyous occasion, but it also carries legal implications for your estate. A civil partnership is a legally recognized relationship between two individuals, offering legal and financial protections similar to marriage, but without the religious or traditional connotations associated with marriage. Your spouse or partner may become the primary beneficiary of your assets, and you may want to provide for them in a more comprehensive manner than you did before. Reviewing your will and updating it to reflect your new marital status is crucial to ensure your spouse or partner is adequately protected in the event of your passing.

Additionally, you may wish to specify how your assets should be distributed in the event of both you and your spouse's untimely demise. For example, if you have children from a previous relationship or if you wish to include charitable donations, updating your will to address these considerations is essential.

2. Welcoming Children or Grandchildren

The birth or adoption of a child or grandchild is a momentous occasion. It brings joy, love, and increased responsibility. You'll want to update your will to name guardians for your children and establish trusts or other provisions to provide for their financial well-being. Failing to do so could result in the court making these decisions on your behalf, which may not align with your intentions.

3. Divorce or Separation

Conversely, the dissolution of a marriage or partnership can have a profound impact on your estate planning. You may want to revise your will to remove your former spouse or partner as a beneficiary, trustee, or executor. Failing to do so could result in your ex-spouse benefiting from your estate or making crucial decisions regarding your assets.

4. Acquiring or Selling Assets

Life is a continuous journey of acquiring and divesting assets. Whether you inherit property, buy a new home, or sell a business, your financial circumstances evolve. These changes can affect your estate's value and composition, making it essential to adjust your will accordingly. Failure to update your will might lead to unintended consequences or disputes among your heirs.

5. Changing Financial Situations

Fluctuations in your financial circumstances can also necessitate updates to your will. A significant increase or decrease in your wealth may prompt you to reconsider your distribution plan. You may want to reassess charitable giving, establish trusts to protect your assets, or adjust provisions for specific beneficiaries based on their financial needs.

The Dynamics of Family Relationships

Family dynamics play a pivotal role in estate planning. The intricate relationships among family members can influence your decisions and require careful consideration. Let's explore various family-related scenarios that underscore the importance of keeping your will current.

1. Blended Families

In today's society, blended families are increasingly common. These families may consist of stepchildren, half-siblings, and multiple sets of parents. When drafting or updating your will, you must navigate the complexities of blended family dynamics. Failing to address these relationships can lead to confusion, resentment, and legal challenges after your passing.

It is essential to clearly specify how you wish to provide for all members of your blended family, ensuring that each individual is treated fairly and equitably according to your intentions. This might involve creating trusts, designating specific assets, or outlining your expectations for your executor to manage any potential conflicts.

2. Estranged Family Members

Family disputes can sometimes lead to estrangement between individuals. If you have estranged family members, it's crucial to address their status in your will explicitly. This may involve excluding them from your estate, setting conditions for their inheritance, or offering them a nominal gift to minimize the chances of a legal challenge. By doing so, you can mitigate the potential for disputes and ensure your assets are distributed according to your wishes.

3. Changes in Beneficiary Relationships

Relationships with beneficiaries can evolve over time. You may become closer to certain family members or friends, or you may want to provide additional support for a beneficiary due to unforeseen circumstances. Regularly reviewing and updating your will allows you to adapt to these changing dynamics, ensuring your assets are distributed as you intended.

4. Consideration for Special Needs Beneficiaries

If you have a beneficiary with special needs, such as a disabled child or dependent, your will should reflect your commitment to their well-being. Establishing a special needs trust can safeguard their financial future without jeopardizing their eligibility for government assistance programs. Regular updates to this trust will help ensure it aligns with your beneficiary's evolving needs and circumstances.

The Importance of Regular Updates

Estate planning isn't a one-and-done task. Instead, it's an ongoing process that should evolve alongside your life and family dynamics. Here are some reasons why regular updates to your will are paramount:

1. Legal Compliance

Laws surrounding wills, trusts, and estates can change over time. Failing to update your will to comply with new legal requirements may render it invalid or lead to unintended consequences. Regular updates ensure your estate plan remains legally sound.

2. Avoiding Family Conflicts

An outdated will can create confusion and animosity among family members. Prevent disputes and maintain family harmony by clearly articulating your intentions in your updated will.

3. Protecting Vulnerable Beneficiaries

As mentioned earlier, special needs beneficiaries require ongoing support and care. Regular updates to their trust ensure they continue to receive the necessary financial assistance and protection they need.

4. Keeping Up with Financial Changes

Your financial situation may change significantly over time. Updating your will helps you make the most of your assets and adapt your plan to changing circumstances.

5. Reflecting Your Current Wishes

Life experiences and personal values can evolve. Your current wishes may differ from those expressed in an outdated will. Updating your will ensures that your legacy aligns with your present beliefs and priorities.

6. Avoiding Unintended Consequences

Failure to update your will can lead to unintended beneficiaries receiving your assets. Regularly reviewing and revising your will minimizes the risk of these undesired outcomes.

Conclusion

Estate planning is an ongoing journey that requires vigilance and adaptability. Life events and family dynamics are in a constant state of flux, making it imperative to revisit and update your will regularly. By doing so, you can ensure that your final wishes are current, legally valid, and reflective of your evolving circumstances.

The process of updating your will need not be daunting. Seek guidance from legal professionals who specialize in estate planning to help you navigate the intricacies of changing life circumstances and family dynamics. In the end, your efforts in keeping your will up-to-date will provide peace of mind, clarity, and the assurance that your loved ones will be well cared for according to your wishes when the time comes.

Introduction

Estate planning is a comprehensive process that involves making critical decisions to protect your assets and loved ones in the event of your passing. Among these decisions, perhaps one of the most significant and emotionally charged is the appointment of guardians for your minor children. This choice can be a source of comfort, ensuring that your children are cared for by someone you trust, or it can lead to disputes and conflicts if not handled properly. In this article, we will explore the process of choosing guardians for minor children and provide guidance on navigating potential disputes.

Understanding Guardianship

Before diving into the complexities of choosing guardians and handling disputes, it's essential to have a clear understanding of what guardianship for minors entails.

1. Definition of Guardianship

Guardianship is a legal arrangement where a responsible adult is appointed to make decisions for and take care of a minor child when their biological or adoptive parents are unable to do so. These circumstances may arise due to the parents' death, incapacity, or other reasons preventing them from fulfilling their parental duties.

Guardians can be broadly categorized into two types:

Guardian of the Person: This individual is responsible for the child's day-to-day care, including housing, education, healthcare, and emotional well-being.

Guardian of the Estate: This person is tasked with managing the child's financial affairs, such as inheritance, investments, and property, until the child reaches the age of majority.

The Importance of Choosing Guardians

Selecting guardians for your minor children is a crucial aspect of estate planning for several reasons.

1. Protecting Your Child's Welfare

By appointing guardians, you ensure that your children will have a stable and caring environment in the event of your untimely demise. This step helps safeguard their physical, emotional, and financial well-being.

2. Avoiding Court Intervention

If you do not name guardians in your estate plan, the court will step in to make this decision. Court proceedings can be time-consuming, costly, and may result in guardianship arrangements that do not align with your wishes.

3. Maintaining Family Unity

Choosing guardians allows you to select individuals who share your values, beliefs, and parenting style. This helps maintain family unity and ensures that your children are raised in a familiar environment.

The Process of Choosing Guardians

Selecting guardians for your minor children is a deeply personal decision, and several factors should be considered during this process.

1. Identifying Potential Guardians

Start by identifying potential guardians within your family or close circle of friends. Consider individuals who are willing and able to take on the responsibilities of guardianship.

2. Assessing Qualifications

Evaluate the potential guardians based on their ability to provide a stable and loving home, financial stability, parenting skills, and shared values with your family.

3. Open Communication

Engage in open and honest discussions with the chosen guardians to ensure they are willing to accept this responsibility and understand your expectations.

4. Contingency Plans

Consider naming alternate guardians in case your primary choices are unable or unwilling to assume the role when the need arises.

5. Legal Documentation

Consult with an experienced estate planning attorney to draft the necessary legal documents, such as a will and/or a guardianship designation, to formalize your choices.

Navigating Potential Disputes

While choosing guardians for your minor children is a significant decision, it can also be a source of contention among family members. Here are some strategies for navigating potential disputes:

1. Open Communication

Clear and open communication is key to preventing and resolving disputes. Discuss your choices with family members and explain your reasoning to help them understand your decision.

2. Seek Mediation

If disputes arise, consider engaging the services of a mediator who can help facilitate discussions and find common ground among concerned parties.

3. Put the Child's Interests First

Remind all parties involved that the ultimate goal is to protect the child's best interests. Emphasize that the chosen guardians are people you trust to provide a loving and stable environment.

4. Document Your Intentions

Include a detailed explanation of your guardian selection in your estate planning documents. This can help clarify your intentions and minimize misunderstandings.

5. Professional Guidance

Consult with an attorney who specializes in estate planning and family law to ensure that your documents are legally sound and enforceable.

Potential Challenges and Solutions

While many guardianship arrangements proceed smoothly, challenges may still arise. It's essential to be aware of potential issues and how to address them.

1. Relocation

Guardians may need to relocate for various reasons, such as job opportunities. To address this, include provisions in your estate plan that allow for flexibility in the guardianship arrangement, or consider naming co-guardians who can share responsibilities.

2. Changes in Circumstances

Life is unpredictable, and guardians may experience changes in their financial, health, or personal circumstances. Regularly review and update your estate plan to account for these changes and make necessary adjustments to guardianship arrangements.

3. Family Dynamics

Family dynamics can evolve over time, leading to strained relationships between guardians and other family members. Open communication and mediation can help mitigate conflicts, but it's essential to be prepared for potential family tensions.

4. Legal Challenges

In some cases, disgruntled family members may contest your choice of guardians in court. To minimize the likelihood of legal challenges, work closely with an attorney to ensure your documents are clear, well-drafted, and legally sound.

Conclusion

Choosing guardians for your minor children is a pivotal aspect of estate planning, one that should be approached with care and consideration. By understanding the importance of guardianship, carefully selecting guardians, and addressing potential disputes, you can ensure that your children's well-being remains a top priority. Estate planning, including the appointment of guardians, is a proactive step that provides peace of mind and security for your family's future.

Introduction

In the intricate web of estate planning, the decision to disinherit or provide unequal shares to family members is a daunting one. The emotional and legal complexities surrounding this choice can be profound, shaping the dynamics of family relationships for generations to come. This article delves into the intricacies of disinheriting heirs, exploring the emotional toll it takes on both testators (who create and legally execute a will) and beneficiaries, while also unraveling the legal framework that governs such decisions. By the end, you will have a comprehensive understanding of the factors to consider and the steps to take when facing this challenging aspect of estate planning.

The Decision to Disinherit: Emotional Complexity

Disinheriting an heir is a decision fraught with emotional turmoil. It's a choice that often arises from deep-seated family conflicts, resentment, or estrangement. Here, we explore the various emotional dimensions that make this decision so challenging.

1. Family Discord and Estrangement

One of the most common reasons for disinheriting heirs is a history of family discord and estrangement. Deep-rooted conflicts, grudges, or unresolved issues can lead a testator to exclude a family member from their will. The emotional toll of such estrangement on both parties can be immense, causing pain, anger, and regret.

2. Financial Irresponsibility

Sometimes, a testator may choose to disinherit an heir due to concerns about financial irresponsibility. They may worry that leaving a significant inheritance to a financially reckless family member could lead to squandering of assets or irresponsible behavior. The emotional conflict in such cases stems from the desire to protect the family's wealth while also grappling with the consequences of excluding a loved one.

3. Black Sheep Syndrome

The "black sheep" of a family, often seen as the troublemaker or outlier, can create significant emotional turmoil for the testator. The term "black sheep" of a family refers to a family member who is seen as different, wayward, or disreputable compared to the rest of the family, often due to their behavior, beliefs, or choices. The decision to disinherit a black sheep may be motivated by concerns about their impact on the family's financial stability or reputation. However, it can be a heavy emotional burden, as the testator must confront the isolation of their own kin.

Legal Aspects of Disinheriting Heirs

While the emotional dimensions of disinheriting heirs are profound, there is also a complex legal framework that dictates how such decisions are executed and upheld. Understanding the legal aspects is essential when considering this course of action.

1. Testamentary Freedom

In many jurisdictions, individuals have the legal right to decide how their assets are distributed after their death. This principle of testamentary freedom allows testators to choose their heirs and allocate their assets according to their wishes. However, there are legal limitations to this freedom, such as spousal and dependent rights, which may vary by jurisdiction.

2. Providing a Reason

In some jurisdictions, it is advisable, though not always legally required, for testators to provide a reason for disinheriting an heir in their will. This serves as a precautionary measure to avoid potential legal challenges from disinherited beneficiaries. Clearly articulating the rationale behind the decision can help deter claims of undue influence or incapacity.

3. Legal Challenges and Family Provision Acts

Disinheriting an heir can lead to legal challenges. Many jurisdictions have Family Provision Acts or similar legislation that allows disinherited heirs to contest a will on the grounds of inadequate provision or unfair treatment. Courts may consider the financial needs of the disinherited heir and whether the testator had a moral duty to provide for them.

4. Undue Influence and Capacity

To ensure the validity of a will, it must be established that the testator executed it with full mental capacity and without undue influence. In cases where an heir is disinherited, allegations of undue influence or the testator's lack of capacity can arise, leading to legal disputes. It is crucial for testators to take measures to safeguard against such challenges.

Alternatives to Disinheritance

Disinheriting heirs is not the only option available to testators facing complex family dynamics or concerns. There are alternative approaches that may help achieve desired outcomes while preserving family relationships to some extent.

1. Conditional Bequests

Rather than outright disinheriting an heir, testators can make bequests conditional on specific behaviors or circumstances. For instance, an heir might receive their inheritance only if they meet certain conditions, such as completing a college degree, maintaining stable employment, or seeking counseling to resolve family issues.

2. Lifetime Gifts and Trusts

Testators can choose to provide financial support to heirs during their lifetime, bypassing the traditional inheritance process. This can be achieved through gifts or the establishment of trusts that provide controlled access to funds. Such arrangements allow testators to support family members while mitigating concerns about mismanagement of assets.

3. Open Communication

One of the most effective alternatives to disinheriting heirs is open and honest communication. Family meetings or discussions facilitated by estate planning professionals can help address underlying issues, express concerns, and find mutually agreeable solutions. Mediation can be a valuable tool to mend fractured relationships within the family.

The Role of Estate Planning Professionals

Navigating the emotional and legal complexities of disinheriting heirs requires professional guidance. Estate planning professionals play a vital role in assisting testators in making informed decisions and executing their wishes effectively.

1. Legal Counsel

Estate planning attorneys are well-versed in the legal intricacies of wills and estates. They can help testators draft clear and legally sound documents, minimizing the risk of legal challenges. Additionally, they can advise on the specific laws and regulations governing disinheriting heirs in the relevant jurisdiction.

2. Financial Advisors

Financial advisors can assist in crafting alternative financial strategies that align with the testator's goals. They can help explore options like lifetime gifts, trusts, or other financial vehicles that protect assets while providing for family members.

3. Mediation and Counseling

Mediators and family counselors can facilitate difficult conversations within the family. Their expertise in conflict resolution can be invaluable in addressing underlying issues and helping families arrive at mutually acceptable solutions, potentially averting the need for disinheriting heirs.

Conclusion

Disinheriting heirs is a deeply personal and legally complex aspect of estate planning. The emotional toll it takes on both testators and beneficiaries is undeniable, and the legal framework governing such decisions is intricate. As testators grapple with the difficult choice of disinheriting or providing unequal shares to family members, it is essential to seek professional guidance and consider alternatives that may preserve family harmony while achieving desired outcomes. Ultimately, open communication, thoughtful planning, and careful consideration of the emotional and legal complexities are key to navigating this challenging aspect of estate planning successfully.

Introduction

The process of estate planning is a vital aspect of one's financial and personal life. It involves making crucial decisions about how your assets will be distributed after your demise. One of the key elements of estate planning is the selection of an executor. The executor plays a critical role in managing your estate, ensuring that your wishes are carried out, and resolving conflicts that may arise during the probate process. In this article, we will delve into the importance of executor selection and the responsibilities that come with this role, while also shedding light on the potential consequences of making the wrong choice.

The Role of an Executor

An executor is a person or entity appointed to oversee the administration of an individual's estate after they pass away. This role is pivotal, as the executor is responsible for ensuring that the deceased person's wishes, as outlined in their will, are carried out efficiently and accurately. Here are some primary responsibilities of an executor:

Locating and Managing Assets: Executors must locate, safeguard, and manage the deceased person's assets. This includes real estate, investments, bank accounts, personal property, and more. Proper management ensures that the assets maintain their value during the probate process.

Probate Proceedings: Executors initiate and navigate the probate process, which involves validating the will, paying off debts and taxes, and distributing assets to beneficiaries. This can be a complex legal procedure, and the executor must ensure all steps are followed meticulously.

Communication and Documentation: Executors are responsible for notifying beneficiaries and creditors of the deceased's passing, as well as maintaining detailed records of all financial transactions related to the estate. Transparent communication is crucial to avoid misunderstandings and disputes.

Debt Settlement: Executors must identify and settle any outstanding debts or obligations of the deceased. This includes paying creditors and resolving any legal disputes that may arise.

Asset Distribution: One of the primary duties of an executor is to distribute assets to the beneficiaries as specified in the will. This must be done fairly and in accordance with the deceased person's wishes.

Tax Compliance: Executors are responsible for ensuring that all necessary tax filings are completed accurately and on time. This includes income tax returns for the deceased person and estate tax returns if applicable.

Managing Estate Expenses: Executors may need to cover certain estate expenses, such as legal fees, funeral costs, and maintenance of real estate, using funds from the estate.

Selecting the Right Executor

Choosing the right executor is a critical decision in the estate planning process. The following factors should be considered when selecting an executor:

Trustworthiness and Integrity: An executor should be someone you trust implicitly. They will have access to sensitive financial information and the power to make important decisions on your behalf.

Organizational Skills: Estate administration involves a significant amount of paperwork and record-keeping. An executor should be organized and capable of managing these responsibilities efficiently.

Financial Literacy: It's beneficial if the executor has a good understanding of financial matters, as they will be responsible for managing assets, paying debts, and ensuring proper tax compliance.

Availability: The executor should be willing and able to commit the time required to fulfill their responsibilities. Estate administration can be time-consuming, and an absentee or unavailable executor can lead to delays and complications.

Neutrality: If there is potential for family conflicts or disputes among beneficiaries, it may be wise to select an executor who can remain neutral and make impartial decisions.

Experience or Professional Assistance: Executors with prior experience in estate administration or legal and financial expertise can be highly valuable. Alternatively, you can appoint a professional, such as an attorney or financial advisor, to assist in the process.

Geographic Proximity: Choosing an executor who resides nearby can be advantageous, as they can more easily handle day-to-day responsibilities, attend court hearings, and meet with professionals involved in estate administration.

The Consequences of Choosing the Wrong Executor

Selecting the wrong executor can have far-reaching consequences for your estate and beneficiaries. Here are some potential pitfalls:

Conflict Among Beneficiaries: A poorly chosen executor may lack the skills or temperament to mediate conflicts among beneficiaries. This can lead to disputes, legal battles, and strained family relationships.

Financial Mismanagement: Incompetent or negligent executors may mishandle estate assets, resulting in financial losses for beneficiaries. This can be particularly devastating if the estate includes valuable assets or investments.

Legal Liabilities: Executors who fail to fulfill their duties properly may face legal consequences, including personal liability for financial losses suffered by the estate or its beneficiaries.

Delays in Estate Settlement: An executor who lacks organization or commitment can cause significant delays in settling the estate. This can be frustrating for beneficiaries who may depend on their inheritance.

Tax Consequences: Inadequate tax planning and compliance can lead to unnecessary tax burdens on the estate or beneficiaries. A knowledgeable executor is essential for minimizing tax liabilities.

Loss of Assets: In extreme cases, a dishonest or unscrupulous executor may embezzle or misappropriate estate assets for personal gain, resulting in substantial losses for beneficiaries.

Alternatives to Individual Executors

While many people choose individual family members or trusted friends as their executors, it's essential to be aware of alternative options.

Professional Executors: Hiring a professional executor, such as an attorney or a financial institution, can be a wise choice for complex estates or when there is a lack of suitable individuals. These professionals have the expertise to navigate the legal and financial aspects of estate administration.

Co-Executors: If you have difficulty choosing a single executor, you can appoint co-executors who share the responsibilities. This can help distribute the workload and provide checks and balances.

Successor Executors: It's crucial to name a successor executor in case your primary choice is unable or unwilling to fulfill the role when the time comes. This ensures that there is always someone ready to step in.

Executor Advisors: If you have a trusted friend or family member who may not be suitable as the primary executor but has valuable insights, you can appoint them as an advisor to work alongside the executor.

Communication and Transparency

Regardless of who you select as your executor, clear communication and transparency are key to a successful estate administration. Here are some tips to facilitate this:

Open Dialogue: Discuss your wishes and expectations with your chosen executor before including them in your will. This will help them understand their responsibilities and your intentions.

Document Everything: Maintain detailed records of your assets, debts, and estate planning documents. Share this information with your executor so they have a comprehensive understanding of your financial affairs.

Regular Updates: Keep your executor informed about any changes in your estate plan, such as updates to your will or the acquisition of new assets. Ensure that your executor knows where to find important documents.

Professional Guidance: Encourage your executor to seek professional advice when necessary. Complex legal or financial matters may require the expertise of lawyers, accountants, or financial advisors.

Conclusion

Selecting the right executor and clearly defining their responsibilities is a critical component of effective estate planning. The executor plays a pivotal role in ensuring that your wishes are carried out, debts are settled, and assets are distributed according to your intentions. Conversely, choosing the wrong executor can lead to conflicts, financial mismanagement, and legal issues that can be burdensome for your loved ones.

When making this important decision, consider the qualities and qualifications that make an individual or entity suitable for the role. Whether you choose a trusted family member, a professional executor, or a combination of both, communication and transparency are key to a smooth and successful estate administration.

In the end, thoughtful executor selection and clear communication can provide peace of mind, knowing that your estate will be managed responsibly and in accordance with your wishes, ultimately facilitating a smoother transition for your beneficiaries during a challenging time.

Introduction

In the intricate tapestry of estate planning and inheritance, the probate process occupies a central role. It is the legal mechanism through which the assets of a deceased person are distributed to their beneficiaries and heirs. While probate serves an essential purpose in ensuring a fair and orderly transfer of assets, it can also be a complex and potentially lengthy procedure. In this comprehensive guide, we will explore the probate process in detail, shedding light on its impact on asset distribution and highlighting potential delays that may arise.

What is Probate?

Probate is the legal process that validates a deceased person's will and oversees the distribution of their assets to designated beneficiaries or heirs. This process is typically overseen by a court, which ensures that the deceased's wishes, as outlined in their will, are carried out correctly. If there is no will, the court will follow the state's intestacy laws to determine how the assets should be distributed.

Probate involves several key steps, each of which plays a critical role in the asset distribution process. Understanding these steps is essential for anyone involved in estate planning or dealing with the aftermath of a loved one's passing.

Step 1: Initiating Probate

The probate process begins when someone with a legal interest in the deceased person's estate, often an executor named in the will, files a petition with the local probate court. This petition typically includes the deceased's will and a death certificate. Once the court receives these documents, it officially opens the probate case.

Step 2: Appointment of Executor or Personal Representative

One of the early decisions in the probate process is the appointment of an executor or personal representative. This individual is responsible for managing the deceased's estate during probate, including locating and valuing assets, paying debts and taxes, and distributing assets to beneficiaries as specified in the will. If the deceased did not name an executor in their will, the court will appoint one.

Step 3: Asset Inventory and Appraisal

A critical aspect of the probate process is determining the value of the deceased person's assets. This involves identifying all assets subject to probate, such as real estate, bank accounts, investments, and personal property. Appraisers may be hired to assess the value of certain assets, ensuring that they are accurately accounted for in the estate.

Step 4: Notification of Creditors and Debts

During probate, the executor must notify known creditors of the deceased person's passing. This notification provides creditors with an opportunity to make claims against the estate for any outstanding debts. The executor is responsible for reviewing and approving or denying these claims based on their validity and the available assets.

Step 5: Payment of Debts and Taxes

Before distributing assets to beneficiaries, the estate's debts and taxes must be paid. This includes outstanding loans, medical bills, and any federal or state estate taxes that may apply. The executor uses the estate's assets to cover these obligations.

Step 6: Asset Distribution

Once all debts and taxes have been satisfied, the executor can begin the process of distributing the remaining assets to the beneficiaries according to the terms of the will. This is the culmination of the probate process and the moment when the deceased's wishes are realized.

The Impact of Probate on Asset Distribution

Probate plays a pivotal role in asset distribution, ensuring that a deceased person's wishes are honored and their estate is settled correctly. However, it's important to recognize the impact that probate can have on this process, both positive and negative.

1. Positive Aspects of Probate on Asset Distribution

Legal Validation: Probate provides a legally recognized framework for validating the deceased person's will. This ensures that the distribution of assets is done in accordance with their expressed wishes, reducing the potential for disputes among beneficiaries.

Creditor Notification: Probate requires creditors to come forward with their claims within a specified timeframe. This protects beneficiaries from surprise debts and allows for a fair evaluation of outstanding obligations.

Clear Process: Probate establishes a clear and structured process for settling an estate. This can be particularly beneficial when dealing with complex estates or situations where multiple parties have a claim to the assets.

2. Potential Delays in Asset Distribution Due to Probate

While probate offers important protections, it can also introduce delays and complications into the asset distribution process.

Time: Probate can be a time-consuming process, often taking several months to several years to complete, depending on the complexity of the estate and local regulations. During this time, beneficiaries may experience financial stress as they wait for their inheritances.

Costs: The probate process involves various fees, including court costs, attorney fees, and appraiser fees. These expenses can diminish the overall value of the estate and reduce the inheritances received by beneficiaries.

Public Record: Probate is a public process, meaning that the details of the deceased person's estate, including asset values and the names of beneficiaries, become a matter of public record. Some individuals prefer to keep their financial affairs private, which is not possible in probate.

Potential for Disputes: While probate aims to resolve disputes, it can also be a breeding ground for conflicts among beneficiaries or between beneficiaries and the executor. Disagreements over asset distribution or the validity of the will can lead to litigation, further delaying the process.

Strategies to Mitigate Delays in Probate

Given the potential delays and complexities associated with probate, individuals and estate planners often explore strategies to mitigate these challenges. Here are some approaches to consider:

1. Estate Planning

Effective estate planning can help minimize the impact of probate on asset distribution. Strategies may include:

Creating a Living Trust: Assets placed in a living trust are typically not subject to probate, allowing for a quicker and more private distribution to beneficiaries.

Updating Beneficiary Designations: Assets with designated beneficiaries, such as life insurance policies and retirement accounts, can pass directly to the named beneficiaries outside of probate.

Gifts and Annual Exclusions: Individuals can gift assets during their lifetime, reducing the overall size of their estate subject to probate.

2. Joint Ownership

Holding assets jointly with right of survivorship can expedite asset transfer outside of probate. When one joint owner passes away, ownership of the asset automatically transfers to the surviving owner.

3. Small Estate Procedures

In some jurisdictions, small estates with relatively low values may qualify for simplified probate procedures, which can reduce the time and cost associated with the process.

4. Communication and Mediation

Clear communication among beneficiaries and between beneficiaries and the executor can help prevent disputes that might lead to delays and litigation. Mediation can be a valuable tool in resolving conflicts amicably.

5. Professional Guidance

Working with an experienced estate attorney can help navigate the probate process efficiently. They can provide guidance on legal requirements, deadlines, and strategies for minimizing delays.

Conclusion

The probate process is a fundamental aspect of estate planning and asset distribution. While it serves the critical function of ensuring the deceased person's wishes are honored and debts are paid, it can also introduce delays and expenses. Understanding the impact of probate on asset distribution and the strategies available to mitigate potential delays is essential for individuals seeking to secure their legacies and for those responsible for executing their wills. By carefully considering the options and seeking professional guidance when needed, individuals can work towards a smoother and more efficient probate process, ultimately providing for their loved ones in the manner they intended.

Introduction

Estate planning is a crucial aspect of financial and familial well-being. It ensures that your assets are distributed according to your wishes after your passing, providing financial security for your loved ones. However, even with the best intentions and a meticulously crafted will, conflicts can arise among beneficiaries when it comes to the distribution of assets. In this comprehensive guide, we will explore common disputes that can arise among beneficiaries and effective strategies for resolution.

Understanding the Nature of Beneficiary Conflicts

Beneficiary conflicts within estate wills can be emotionally charged and complex. These disputes often stem from a combination of financial, emotional, and interpersonal factors. To effectively resolve these conflicts, it's important to understand the underlying dynamics and motivations that drive them.

1. Unequal Distribution of Assets

One of the most common causes of beneficiary conflict is an unequal distribution of assets among heirs. This can happen for various reasons, including personal relationships, perceived needs, or special considerations for certain beneficiaries.

Resolution: To address this conflict, open and transparent communication is essential. The testator (the person creating the will) should consider discussing their intentions with beneficiaries to avoid surprises. If conflicts persist, engaging a mediator or estate planning attorney can help find a fair compromise.

2. Disputed Validity of the Will

Sometimes, beneficiaries may dispute the validity of the will itself. They may question the testator's mental capacity, allege undue influence, or claim that the will is a result of fraud.

Resolution: When a will's validity is contested, it's crucial to follow legal procedures. Courts will review evidence and testimonies to determine the will's legitimacy. Seeking legal counsel is essential for both beneficiaries and executors to ensure a fair and lawful resolution.

3. Ambiguity in the Will

Ambiguity in a will's language can lead to confusion and disagreements among beneficiaries. Vague terms or unclear instructions can create fertile ground for disputes.

Resolution: In such cases, consulting with an estate attorney is advisable. The court may interpret the ambiguous clauses, striving to honor the testator's intent. It's essential to emphasize the importance of clear and concise language in will drafting to prevent future conflicts.

4. Executor Disputes

Beneficiaries may not always agree on the choice of the executor responsible for administering the estate. Conflict can arise when beneficiaries doubt the executor's ability, fairness, or intentions.

Resolution: Ideally, the testator should choose an executor whom beneficiaries trust and respect. However, if disputes persist, beneficiaries can petition the court to remove or replace the executor. Mediation may also help resolve differences and restore trust in the executor's actions.

5. Delay in Estate Settlement

Beneficiaries may become frustrated and contentious if the estate settlement process is prolonged. Delays can result from various factors, including legal complexities, asset appraisal, or disputes among beneficiaries.

Resolution: To expedite the process, the executor should communicate regularly with beneficiaries, explaining the reasons for delays and outlining a realistic timeline. Mediation or arbitration can also help resolve conflicts related to delays, ensuring a smoother distribution of assets.

Effective Conflict Resolution Strategies

Now that we have identified common beneficiary conflicts in estate wills, let's explore strategies for resolving these disputes amicably.

1. Open and Transparent Communication

Effective communication is the cornerstone of conflict resolution. Beneficiaries should be encouraged to express their concerns, questions, and expectations. Testators can play a pivotal role in this process by sharing their intentions and the reasoning behind asset distribution decisions.

2. Mediation and Arbitration

Mediation and arbitration are alternative dispute resolution methods that can be highly effective in resolving beneficiary conflicts. A neutral third party can facilitate discussions and guide beneficiaries toward a mutually agreeable solution.

3. Legal Counsel

Beneficiaries and executors should seek legal counsel when conflicts escalate or involve complex legal issues. Estate attorneys can provide guidance, represent their clients' interests, and ensure that the process follows legal procedures.

4. Fairness and Equity

Testators should strive to create wills that are perceived as fair and equitable by beneficiaries. Addressing concerns and providing explanations can help prevent disputes before they arise.

5. Amending the Will

If beneficiaries unanimously agree to amend the will to address their concerns, it is legally possible to do so, provided the testator is still alive and mentally competent. Consulting with an estate attorney is crucial to ensure the changes are legally valid.

6. Estate Planning Professionals

Engaging professionals, such as financial advisors, estate planners, and mediators, can help navigate complex family dynamics and ensure that the estate plan is comprehensive and well-suited to the family's unique circumstances.

7. Family Meetings

Convening family meetings, facilitated by a neutral party if necessary, can be an effective way to address conflicts, share information, and find common ground. These meetings provide a forum for open discussions and can lead to mutually acceptable solutions.

Case Studies

To illustrate the effectiveness of conflict resolution strategies, let's explore two hypothetical case studies.

Case Study 1: Unequal Distribution

Scenario: Jane, a testator, left the majority of her estate to her eldest son, Michael, believing he needed it the most due to his financial difficulties. This decision caused tension among her other two children, Sarah and David, who felt slighted.

Resolution: Jane could have held a family meeting before her passing to explain her reasoning and address her children's concerns. Additionally, she could have considered leaving sentimental items or heirlooms (cherished family possessions or objects with historical or sentimental value passed down through generations) to Sarah and David to balance the perceived inequality. Mediation between the siblings may help them reach a more equitable agreement.

Scenario: After Richard passed away, his will was contested by his second wife, Susan, who alleged that the will was forged by his children from his first marriage.

Resolution: Susan and Richard's children should consult with estate attorneys to handle the legal aspects of the dispute. The court will review evidence to determine the will's validity. Mediation may also be beneficial to facilitate communication between the parties and explore potential compromises.

Conclusion

Beneficiary conflicts in estate wills are emotionally challenging and can strain family relationships. However, with open communication, mediation, legal guidance, and a commitment to fairness, many conflicts can be resolved amicably. Estate planning professionals play a crucial role in helping families navigate these delicate situations and ensure that the testator's wishes are upheld while preserving family harmony. Ultimately, a well-thought-out estate plan, combined with effective conflict resolution strategies, can help beneficiaries find common ground and move forward with confidence in the distribution of assets.

Introduction

Estate planning is a complex and delicate process, often requiring individuals to make difficult decisions about how their assets will be distributed after their passing. One such decision is the choice to disinherit a potential heir. While the right to disinherit heirs is generally protected by law, it is not without its challenges. This article explores the legal challenges that may arise when heirs contest being disinherited, shedding light on the intricacies of estate wills, conflicts, and their resolutions.

The Right to Disinherit

Before delving into the challenges associated with disinheritance, it is crucial to understand that individuals have the legal right to disinherit anyone from their estate, including close family members and loved ones. This right is a fundamental aspect of testamentary freedom, allowing the testator (the person creating the will) to make decisions about their estate based on their personal preferences and circumstances.

The Principle of Testamentary Freedom

Testamentary freedom is a legal principle that affords individuals the autonomy to determine how their assets will be distributed upon their death. This principle is deeply ingrained in the legal systems of many countries, including the United States. It upholds the idea that a person's wishes regarding their estate should be respected, provided that their will complies with legal requirements.

Legal Challenges to Disinheritance

While the right to disinherit is protected, it is not absolute, and there are specific legal challenges that can arise when heirs contest being disinherited. These challenges often revolve around issues such as the validity of the will, undue influence, lack of capacity, and claims of familial obligations.

1. Validity of the Will

The most common challenge to disinheritance involves questioning the validity of the will itself. A will may be challenged on various grounds, including:

Lack of Formality: Wills must meet certain formal requirements, such as being in writing, signed by the testator, and witnessed by witnesses who are not beneficiaries. If these requirements are not met, the will may be deemed invalid.

Undue Influence: Heirs may claim that the testator was unduly influenced by another party to disinherit them. This could involve allegations of coercion or manipulation, and if proven, can render the will invalid.

Lack of Testamentary Capacity: A testator must have the mental capacity to understand the nature and consequences of their decisions when creating a will. Challenges can arise if it is believed that the testator lacked the mental capacity to make sound decisions at the time the will was executed.

2. Claims of Moral Obligation

In some cases, heirs may argue that they have a moral or ethical right to inherit from the estate, even if they have been disinherited in the will. These claims are typically rooted in the idea that the testator had a moral duty to provide for the heir in question.

Family Maintenance and Support Claims: Some jurisdictions allow family members, particularly spouses and dependent children, to make claims against an estate for maintenance and support. These claims are based on the principle that the testator had a legal obligation to provide for the basic needs of the claimant.

Promissory Estoppel: Promissory estoppel is a legal doctrine that enforces a promise made without formal consideration when it's relied upon and causes detriment to the party who relied on it. In certain situations, heirs may argue that the testator made promises to provide for them in the future, and they relied on these promises to their detriment. This can give rise to claims of promissory estoppel, where the court may enforce the promises made by the testator.

Resolving Challenges to Disinheritance

Resolving challenges to disinheritance can be a lengthy and emotionally draining process for all parties involved. However, it is essential to have mechanisms in place to address these conflicts and ensure that the testator's true intentions are upheld.

1. Mediation and Negotiation

One approach to resolving challenges to disinheritance is through mediation and negotiation. Mediation involves a neutral third party who helps the parties involved reach a mutually agreeable solution. Negotiation allows the parties to discuss their concerns and potentially come to a compromise.

Mediation and negotiation can be advantageous in that they offer a less adversarial and more private way to resolve disputes. They also allow the parties to maintain more control over the outcome compared to going to court.

2. Litigation

When mediation and negotiation fail or when the disputes are particularly contentious, litigation may become necessary. Litigation involves taking the matter to court, where a judge will make a final decision.

Will Contests: Will contests are legal proceedings where heirs challenge the validity of the will. The court will consider evidence and arguments from both sides to determine whether the will should be upheld or invalidated.

Family Maintenance and Support Claims: If an heir is making a claim for family maintenance and support, the court will evaluate the merits of the claim, taking into account the financial needs of the claimant and the resources available in the estate.

3. Proving the Testator's Intent

In many cases, the key to resolving challenges to disinheritance is to establish and prove the testator's true intentions. This may involve presenting evidence such as:

Written Statements: Any written statements or letters from the testator explaining their reasons for disinheriting a particular heir can be valuable evidence in court.

Witness Testimonies: Witnesses who were present when the will was created or who can attest to the testator's capacity and free will are often called upon to provide testimony.

Medical Records: If there are concerns about the testator's mental capacity, medical records and assessments may be used to establish their mental state at the time the will was executed.

Expert Testimonies: In cases involving allegations of undue influence or lack of capacity, experts such as psychologists or psychiatrists may be called upon to provide expert testimony.

4. Considering Alternatives

In some instances, it may be more practical and emotionally beneficial for all parties involved to consider alternative solutions to disinheritance challenges. This could include creating a settlement agreement, establishing a trust for the disinherited heir, or finding other ways to address the heir's needs and concerns.

Conclusion

Disinheriting an heir is a significant decision that can lead to complex legal challenges. While individuals have the right to determine the distribution of their estate, they must navigate the potential obstacles that heirs may pose. Validity issues, claims of undue influence, lack of capacity, and moral obligations can all complicate the process.

Resolving these challenges may involve mediation, negotiation, or litigation, with the goal of proving the testator's true intentions and upholding their wishes. In some cases, alternative solutions that address the needs of disinherited heirs may be a more practical and harmonious approach.

Ultimately, a well-thought-out and legally sound estate plan can help minimize the likelihood of disputes and challenges to disinheritance, ensuring that the wishes of the testator are upheld while also preserving family relationships to the extent possible. Estate planning professionals play a crucial role in guiding individuals through this complex process and helping them make informed decisions that align with their values and goals.

Introduction

Estate disputes can be emotionally and financially draining, tearing apart families and causing irreparable damage to relationships. When a loved one passes away, the last thing one would want is a bitter and protracted legal battle over their estate. While conflicts related to wills are not uncommon, the way in which they are resolved can make a world of difference. In this article, we explore the concept of mediation as an effective and less adversarial approach to resolving estate disputes. Mediation offers several benefits that promote amicable settlements, which are crucial in preserving familial bonds and ensuring a smoother transition of assets after a loved one's passing.

Understanding Estate Disputes

Estate disputes encompass a broad spectrum of conflicts arising in the aftermath of an individual's death. Common issues include disagreements over the distribution of assets, disputes regarding the validity of the will, allegations of undue influence, and concerns about the executor's actions. These conflicts can often be emotionally charged, with family members and beneficiaries grappling with grief, mistrust, and conflicting interests.

The Traditional Adversarial Approach

Traditionally, estate disputes have been resolved through litigation, a process that pits family members against one another in a courtroom setting. This adversarial approach can exacerbate tensions, escalate costs, and prolong the resolution process for years. Moreover, it often results in winners and losers, further damaging relationships within the family.

Mediation as an Alternative

Mediation presents a more humane and collaborative approach to resolving estate disputes. In mediation, a neutral third party, known as the mediator, facilitates communication and negotiation between the parties involved. The goal is to reach a mutually agreeable solution that addresses the concerns and interests of all parties.

Benefits of Mediation in Estate Disputes

1. Preserving Relationships

One of the most significant advantages of mediation in estate disputes is its potential to preserve family relationships. In a courtroom battle, the focus is on winning the case, often at the expense of personal connections. Mediation, on the other hand, encourages open and empathetic communication. It provides a platform for family members to express their feelings, concerns, and aspirations, fostering understanding and empathy among them. This can be invaluable in maintaining familial bonds, which might otherwise be irreparably damaged by a contentious legal battle.

2. Privacy and Confidentiality

Litigation is a public process, with court documents and proceedings often accessible to the public. This lack of privacy can be distressing for families going through the already difficult process of estate dispute resolution. Mediation, in contrast, is a private and confidential process. It allows families to address their issues without the fear of public scrutiny, which can help protect sensitive family matters and personal information.

3. Cost-Effective

Estate litigation can be prohibitively expensive, with legal fees, court costs, and expert witness fees adding up quickly. Mediation is typically a more cost-effective alternative. While there are fees associated with hiring a mediator, they are usually significantly lower than the expenses incurred during litigation. Moreover, the expedited resolution that mediation often offers can further reduce costs, making it a financially prudent choice.

4. Expedited Resolution

Estate disputes can drag on for years in the court system, causing prolonged stress and uncertainty for all parties involved. Mediation, however, is known for its efficiency. With the help of a skilled mediator, families can often reach a resolution more quickly than through the court system. This not only saves time but also allows family members to move forward with their lives and the process of estate distribution sooner.

5. Customized Solutions

In litigation, the outcome is determined by a judge or jury, and the parties have little control over the final decision. Mediation, on the other hand, empowers the parties to craft their own solutions. This means that families can design outcomes that are better tailored to their unique needs and circumstances. This flexibility is especially beneficial in estate disputes, where each family's dynamics and assets are distinct.

6. Reduced Emotional Stress

Estate disputes are emotionally taxing, and the adversarial nature of litigation can amplify this stress. Mediation provides a less confrontational environment where emotions can be addressed constructively. The mediator helps manage emotions and ensures that discussions remain focused on problem-solving rather than personal attacks. This can lead to a more emotionally satisfying resolution for all parties involved.

7. Preservation of Estate Assets

Litigation often results in significant legal fees and costs that can deplete estate assets. In contrast, mediation is a more cost-effective process, which means that a larger portion of the estate's assets can be preserved for distribution to the beneficiaries. This consideration can be particularly important when the estate's value is a point of contention in the dispute.

8. Greater Control

Mediation empowers the parties involved to have a say in the outcome of their dispute. They have the opportunity to voice their concerns, propose solutions, and ultimately make decisions that affect their lives and the distribution of the estate. This sense of control can be empowering and satisfying for family members who may feel disempowered in the traditional litigation process.

Conclusion

Estate disputes are inherently sensitive matters, and the way they are resolved can have lasting consequences for families. Mediation offers a less adversarial, more collaborative, and emotionally supportive approach to addressing these conflicts. By preserving relationships, ensuring privacy, reducing costs, expediting resolution, and allowing for customized solutions, mediation can help families navigate the challenging terrain of estate disputes while minimizing the damage to personal connections. In an already emotionally charged time, mediation offers a path toward harmonious resolutions that honor the wishes of the deceased and maintain the bonds of love and kinship that are so essential to family life. It is a valuable tool in the realm of estate planning, helping families move forward with grace and unity during times of grief and transition.

Introduction

Estate planning is a critical process that involves the distribution of assets, properties, and wealth after a person's demise. When done correctly, it can bring clarity and peace of mind to all parties involved. However, even the most meticulously drafted estate plans can give rise to conflicts and disputes among beneficiaries. In such cases, litigation becomes an avenue for resolving these conflicts. This article explores the potential for beneficiaries to resort to litigation in estate matters and delves into the emotional and financial toll it can take.

Understanding Estate Litigation

Estate litigation encompasses legal disputes arising from the administration, distribution, or interpretation of a deceased person's estate. These disputes can revolve around a variety of issues, including the validity of the will, the proper distribution of assets, allegations of undue influence or fraud, and claims of omitted or disinherited heirs. While it may not be the preferred path for beneficiaries, it often becomes necessary when disagreements cannot be resolved through negotiation or mediation.

The Potential for Beneficiaries to Resort to Litigation

1. Ambiguous or Invalid Wills

One of the primary triggers for estate litigation is the presence of ambiguous or invalid wills. If the will's language is unclear or open to interpretation, beneficiaries may challenge its validity. Additionally, if there are suspicions of fraud or undue influence during the creation of the will, legal action may be initiated to contest its legitimacy.

2. Family Conflict

Estate matters can exacerbate pre-existing family conflicts. Sibling rivalries, past disputes, and longstanding grievances can resurface when beneficiaries perceive an unfair distribution of assets. These disputes can escalate quickly, leading to litigation as the only means of resolution.

3. Omitted Heirs

Sometimes, a deceased person's will may inadvertently omit certain heirs, or there may be questions about the true identity of potential beneficiaries. In such cases, individuals who believe they are entitled to a share of the estate may seek legal redress to assert their rights.

4. Breach of Fiduciary Duty

Fiduciary duty is a legal and ethical obligation that requires individuals or entities, such as trustees, financial advisors, or corporate officers, to act in the best interests of those they serve, often putting the interests of the beneficiary above their own. Estate administrators, executors, and trustees are entrusted with the responsibility of managing and distributing assets in accordance with the deceased's wishes. When beneficiaries suspect a breach of fiduciary duty - such as mismanagement of assets, embezzlement, or conflicts of interest - they may initiate legal proceedings to hold the responsible parties accountable.

The Emotional Toll of Estate Litigation

1. Grief and Loss

Estate litigation often arises during a period of mourning and emotional vulnerability. The loss of a loved one is already a difficult experience, and disputes over inheritance can exacerbate the emotional toll. Beneficiaries may find themselves grappling with grief while simultaneously engaging in legal battles, adding an extra layer of distress.

2. Family Strain

Family dynamics can be profoundly affected by estate litigation. What once was a harmonious relationship among siblings or extended family members can deteriorate rapidly when litigation becomes necessary. The adversarial nature of legal proceedings can lead to estrangement and irreparable damage to family bonds.

3. Delayed Closure

Estate litigation can be a lengthy process, extending the time it takes for beneficiaries to receive their inheritance. This delay in closure can prevent beneficiaries from moving forward with their lives and achieving the sense of finality that comes with settling an estate.

4. Financial Stress

Emotionally draining litigation is often accompanied by substantial legal fees and court costs. Beneficiaries who are involved in estate disputes may find themselves facing unexpected financial burdens. These expenses can further compound the stress and anxiety associated with litigation.

The Financial Toll of Estate Litigation

1. Legal Fees and Costs

Engaging in estate litigation can be expensive. Beneficiaries must hire legal representation, pay court fees, and cover other associated costs. If the dispute continues for an extended period, these expenses can accumulate significantly, depleting the estate's assets meant for distribution.

2. Asset Depletion

Estate litigation can deplete the assets of the estate itself. As legal fees and court costs add up, the estate's value can decrease substantially, leaving less for beneficiaries to inherit. In some cases, the cost of litigation may even exceed the value of the estate, rendering the entire process financially detrimental.

3. Opportunity Cost

The time and resources invested in estate litigation can have a ripple effect on beneficiaries' financial well-being. Legal battles may require beneficiaries to divert their attention from their careers and personal lives, potentially affecting their income and overall financial stability.

4. Strained Relationships

Estate litigation can strain not only familial relationships but also relationships with legal professionals. When beneficiaries feel that their attorneys are not adequately representing their interests or are prolonging the litigation unnecessarily, it can lead to additional legal costs and further financial stress.

Strategies to Avoid or Mitigate Estate Litigation

1. Clear and Comprehensive Estate Planning

The foundation of avoiding estate litigation is a well-drafted, clear, and comprehensive estate plan. Engaging the services of an experienced estate attorney can help ensure that your wishes are clearly articulated in your will or trust, leaving little room for interpretation or dispute.

2. Open Communication

Encouraging open and honest communication among family members can prevent misunderstandings and conflicts. Discussing your estate plan with potential beneficiaries and addressing any concerns they may have can foster understanding and reduce the likelihood of litigation.

3. Use of Mediation

Mediation can be a valuable tool in resolving disputes without resorting to litigation. A skilled mediator can help parties find common ground and reach mutually acceptable solutions. This approach can save time, money, and emotional strain.

4. Professional Fiduciaries

Professional fiduciaries are individuals or entities entrusted to manage the financial and personal affairs of others while upholding a fiduciary duty. Consider appointing a professional fiduciary, such as a corporate trustee or executor, to oversee the administration and distribution of your estate. Their impartiality and expertise can reduce the risk of conflicts of interest and mismanagement of assets.

5. Regularly Update Your Estate Plan

Life circumstances change, and so should your estate plan. Regularly reviewing and updating your plan ensures that it remains relevant and aligned with your current intentions. This can help prevent disputes that may arise from outdated documents.

Conclusion

Estate litigation can have far-reaching consequences, both emotionally and financially, for all parties involved. It can strain relationships, deplete assets, and prolong the closure of an estate. However, with careful estate planning, open communication, and the use of alternative dispute resolution methods like mediation, beneficiaries and families can navigate these challenges and work toward amicable resolutions. Ultimately, the goal of estate planning should be to provide for your loved ones in a way that minimizes the potential for litigation and its often devastating consequences.

Chapter 15. Alternative Dispute Resolution (ADR) Methods

Introduction

In the realm of estate planning and management, conflicts and disputes are not uncommon. The intricacies of wills, inheritances, and estate distribution can lead to disagreements among family members, beneficiaries, and other stakeholders. Traditionally, such conflicts were resolved through courtroom battles, which are not only time-consuming but also emotionally and financially draining. However, there exists a more efficient and amicable path to resolving estate-related disputes: Alternative Dispute Resolution (ADR) methods. In this comprehensive guide, we will explore various ADR methods, such as arbitration and negotiation, and their applications as alternatives to courtroom battles in the context of estate disputes.

Understanding Alternative Dispute Resolution (ADR)

1. The Essence of ADR

Alternative Dispute Resolution, or ADR, encompasses a range of processes and techniques aimed at resolving conflicts outside the traditional court system. These methods prioritize efficiency, confidentiality, and maintaining relationships, making them particularly suitable for estate-related disputes. ADR methods are voluntary, allowing parties to control the outcome and often result in quicker resolutions.

2. Benefits of ADR in Estate Disputes

Cost-Effective: ADR is typically more cost-effective than litigation, as it reduces legal fees, court costs, and other related expenses.

Time-Efficient: Estate matters can drag on in court for years, whereas ADR processes are often swifter, allowing for a quicker resolution.

Preservation of Relationships: ADR methods prioritize preserving relationships among family members and beneficiaries, which is crucial in estate matters.

Confidentiality: ADR proceedings are usually confidential, keeping sensitive family matters out of the public eye.

Exploring ADR Methods

1. Mediation

Mediation is a collaborative ADR method where a neutral third party, known as the mediator, helps disputing parties reach a mutually acceptable resolution. In estate disputes, mediators facilitate discussions among beneficiaries, heirs, or family members to find common ground.

Process: The mediator guides discussions, ensuring that each party has an opportunity to express their concerns and propose solutions. This process can lead to a legally binding agreement.

Benefits: Mediation allows for open communication, often resulting in creative solutions that meet the specific needs and desires of the parties involved.

2. Arbitration

Arbitration is another ADR method in which parties present their case to an arbitrator, who acts as a private judge. The arbitrator's decision, known as an award, is binding and enforceable in court, making it a legally binding alternative to a trial.

Process: Parties present their arguments and evidence to the arbitrator, who then renders a decision. The process is typically faster and less formal than a court trial.

Benefits: Arbitration offers a structured and legally enforceable resolution while avoiding the often lengthy court process.

3. Negotiation

Negotiation is the simplest form of ADR, involving direct discussions between the parties in conflict. It is a flexible and informal method that allows disputants to work out a resolution on their terms.

Process: Parties engage in discussions, often with legal counsel present, to reach a settlement. The outcome is entirely in the hands of the parties involved.

Benefits: Negotiation provides maximum control to the parties, allowing them to craft customized solutions.

4. Collaborative Law

Collaborative law is an ADR method in which parties and their attorneys commit to resolving disputes cooperatively. If the collaborative process fails, the parties must hire new counsel for litigation, incentivizing a successful resolution.

Process: Collaborative law encourages open communication and the sharing of information to find mutually beneficial solutions.

Benefits: This approach promotes cooperation, often leading to quicker and more amicable resolutions.

5. Family Dispute Resolution (FDR)

Specifically tailored for family conflicts, FDR is an ADR method designed to address issues related to divorce, child custody, and, in some cases, estate matters.

Process: Trained mediators or dispute resolution professionals assist family members in resolving disputes related to wills, inheritances, or estate distribution.

Benefits: FDR recognizes the emotional aspects of family conflicts, providing a safe space for discussions and fostering understanding among family members.

Selecting the Right ADR Method for Estate Disputes

1. Factors to Consider

When choosing an ADR method for estate-related conflicts, several factors come into play.

Complexity of the Dispute: The level of complexity in the estate matter may influence the choice of ADR method. Arbitration or mediation may be suitable for complex legal issues, while negotiation might suffice for less intricate disputes.

Emotional Dynamics: Consider the emotional state of the parties involved. Mediation and collaborative law may be more appropriate when preserving relationships is a priority.

Cost and Time Constraints: Assess the budget and time constraints of all parties, as different ADR methods have varying costs and timelines.

Legal Representation: Determine whether legal counsel is necessary for the ADR process, as this can impact the choice of method.

2. Combining ADR Methods

In some cases, a combination of ADR methods may be the most effective approach. For example, parties could start with negotiation and escalate to mediation if an agreement isn't reached. Flexibility in approach can lead to better outcomes.

Case Studies: ADR Success Stories in Estate Disputes

1. The Smith Family Estate

In this case, the Smith family faced a bitter dispute over the distribution of their late father's estate. Instead of heading to court, they opted for mediation. With the guidance of a skilled mediator, the family members were able to address their concerns and emotions openly. After several sessions, they reached a consensus on how to divide the estate assets. The result was not only a fair distribution but also the preservation of family bonds that would have been severely strained through litigation.

The Johnson siblings were locked in a contentious battle over their parents' will. The animosity between them made direct negotiation impossible. As a result, they turned to arbitration, where an experienced arbitrator carefully considered all evidence and arguments presented by both sides. The arbitrator's decision, delivered in a timely manner, provided closure to the dispute and prevented further escalation.

Conclusion

Estate-related conflicts are emotionally charged and can be financially burdensome when taken to court. However, Alternative Dispute Resolution (ADR) methods offer a more efficient and amicable path to resolving these disputes. Mediation, arbitration, negotiation, collaborative law, and family dispute resolution are powerful tools that prioritize open communication, cost-effectiveness, and relationship preservation.

The key to success lies in selecting the most appropriate ADR method based on the complexity of the dispute, emotional dynamics, cost considerations, and the presence of legal representation. Moreover, the flexibility to combine ADR methods can lead to tailored solutions that cater to the unique needs of each estate dispute.

As the legal landscape continues to evolve, ADR methods in estate disputes are becoming increasingly popular. They provide a viable alternative to the adversarial nature of the courtroom, allowing families and stakeholders to find resolution and closure while preserving important relationships. In the world of estate wills, conflicts, and resolutions, ADR methods are indeed a beacon of hope, providing a more civilized and harmonious way to navigate the often tumultuous waters of estate disputes.

Introduction

Estate planning is a complex and often emotionally charged process. It involves making decisions about the distribution of one's assets, ensuring the financial security of loved ones, and addressing various legal and financial aspects of inheritance. While it may seem like a straightforward task, the potential for conflicts and misunderstandings among family members during this process is significant. This is where the importance of clear communication comes into play.

In this article, we will explore the vital role that open and honest family discussions play in preventing conflicts and misunderstandings during estate planning. Clear communication is not only essential for drafting a well-structured will but also for fostering family harmony and ensuring the smooth resolution of estate-related issues.

The Foundation of Estate Planning - A Clear Will

1. The Will as a Roadmap

The cornerstone of any estate plan is the last will and testament. A will serves as a roadmap that outlines your wishes regarding asset distribution, guardianship of minor children, and other crucial matters. However, a poorly drafted or ambiguous will can lead to confusion, disputes, and even legal battles among heirs. To avoid such scenarios, clear and concise communication is imperative.

2. The Hazards of Ambiguity

Ambiguity in a will can create fertile ground for disputes. Vague language, incomplete instructions, or contradictory clauses can leave beneficiaries perplexed and at odds with one another. Without a doubt, the consequences of unclear communication in a will can be emotionally distressing and financially burdensome for the surviving family members.

3. Preventing Confusion through Clarity

To prevent confusion and potential conflicts, it is essential to communicate your intentions with clarity in your will. Seek legal counsel to ensure that the document is legally sound and unambiguous. Be specific about your wishes, detailing who should inherit what and under what circumstances. This level of clarity can significantly reduce the chances of misinterpretation and disputes down the road.

Family Dynamics and Communication

1. The Complexity of Family Dynamics

Family dynamics are unique and often complex. Every family has its history, relationships, and intricacies that can impact estate planning discussions. Sibling rivalries, differing financial situations, and varying degrees of involvement in the family business can all contribute to potential conflicts.

2. The Power of Open Dialogue

One of the most effective ways to navigate these complexities is through open and honest dialogue. Family members should be encouraged to express their thoughts, concerns, and expectations regarding the estate planning process. A safe and respectful environment for discussion can foster understanding and reduce the likelihood of misunderstandings.

3. Early Involvement is Key

Many conflicts in estate planning arise from a lack of early involvement of family members in the process. Keeping your intentions secret until after your passing can lead to shock, resentment, and disputes among heirs. Instead, consider involving your family in discussions about your estate plan early on. This can provide an opportunity to address concerns, answer questions, and ensure that everyone is on the same page.

Equal vs. Fair Distribution

1. The Perception of Fairness

One of the most contentious issues in estate planning is the distribution of assets among beneficiaries. What may seem like an equal distribution to one person may not be perceived as fair by another. This perception of fairness often leads to disputes and strained relationships.

2. Clarifying Your Intentions

Clear communication is crucial in addressing this issue. In your estate planning discussions, articulate the reasoning behind your decisions. Whether you choose to distribute assets equally or based on specific needs and circumstances, explaining your thought process can help family members understand your intentions and reduce resentment.

3. The Role of Mediation

In cases where disagreements persist, consider involving a mediator. A neutral third party can facilitate discussions and help family members reach a compromise that everyone can accept. Mediation can be particularly valuable when emotions run high, and communication breaks down.

Preparing for the Unexpected

1. Contingency Planning

Life is unpredictable, and circumstances can change over time. This is why estate plans should include contingency provisions that account for unforeseen events. Clear communication is essential in preparing for these eventualities.

2. Health Care Directives

Discussing your preferences regarding healthcare decisions in the event of incapacity is vital. Share your wishes regarding medical treatment, life support, and end-of-life care with your loved ones. This ensures that your family is aware of your desires and can make informed decisions on your behalf.

3. Powers of Attorney

Appointing a trusted individual as your power of attorney for financial and healthcare matters requires clear communication. This person will be responsible for making important decisions on your behalf if you are unable to do so. Discuss your expectations and provide them with the necessary information and documentation.

Transparency and Financial Information

1. Financial Transparency

One of the leading causes of family conflicts during estate planning is a lack of financial transparency. Hidden assets, undisclosed debts, or financial surprises can be sources of contention. To prevent such issues, be open about your financial situation with your family.

2. Sharing Information

Share essential financial information with your loved ones, including the location of important documents, bank accounts, investments, and debts. This transparency ensures that your family has a clear picture of your financial affairs, making it easier to settle your estate when the time comes.

3. Avoiding Unpleasant Surprises

By providing this information in advance, you can prevent surprises and misunderstandings after your passing. A lack of transparency can lead to suspicions and disputes among heirs, which can be emotionally taxing and time-consuming to resolve.

The Emotional Toll of Miscommunication

1. Impact on Family Relationships

Miscommunication and conflicts during estate planning can have a profound impact on family relationships. The emotional toll of disputes and misunderstandings can lead to long-lasting rifts among siblings and other relatives. These fractures can be difficult, if not impossible, to mend.

2. Legacy Preservation

In addition to preserving your financial legacy, consider the preservation of your emotional legacy. Clear communication during estate planning can ensure that your family remembers you not for the conflicts that arose but for your wisdom, compassion, and thoughtfulness in addressing these matters.

3. The Value of Professional Guidance

Sometimes, the emotional weight of estate planning discussions can be too much for families to handle on their own. In such cases, seeking professional guidance, such as family therapists or counselors, can be invaluable in promoting healthy communication and conflict resolution.

The Legal Consequences of Poor Communication

1. Legal Battles and Expenses

When communication breaks down during estate planning, it can lead to costly legal battles. Heirs may resort to litigation to resolve disputes over asset distribution, guardianship, or the validity of the will. These legal proceedings can deplete the estate's assets and prolong the settlement process.

2. Delayed Resolution

A lack of clear communication can also result in delayed resolution of estate matters. Legal disputes and conflicts can tie up assets and create uncertainty for beneficiaries. A process that could have been relatively straightforward with effective communication can drag on for years in court.

3. Avoidable Stress

The stress and emotional strain of legal battles can be avoided through open and honest communication. By addressing potential conflicts and misunderstandings upfront, you can minimize the risk of legal disputes and the associated stress on your family.

Conclusion

Estate planning is not solely about the distribution of assets; it is also about preserving family relationships and ensuring that your legacy is remembered positively. Clear communication is the linchpin of a successful estate plan. By openly discussing your wishes, intentions, and expectations with your loved ones, you can prevent conflicts, misunderstandings, and legal battles.

Remember that estate planning is an ongoing process. Regularly revisit and update your plan to reflect changing circumstances, and continue to engage in open and honest communication with your family. By doing so, you can create a legacy of harmony, understanding, and financial security for generations to come.

Chapter 17. Professional Guidance in Estate Planning

Introduction

Estate planning is a critical aspect of financial and familial well-being. It is a comprehensive process that involves making decisions about the distribution of your assets and the care of your loved ones after your passing. While the concept of estate planning may seem straightforward, the reality is often far more complex. To navigate the intricate web of legal, financial, and emotional considerations, seeking professional guidance is not just advisable - it's essential.

In this article, we will explore the significance of professional guidance in estate planning and how it plays a pivotal role in crafting a well-structured will while minimizing conflicts among heirs and beneficiaries. We will delve into the various aspects of estate planning that necessitate expert assistance and emphasize the benefits of collaborating with legal and financial professionals.

Understanding the Complexities of Estate Planning

Estate planning goes far beyond merely creating a will. It encompasses a wide range of financial, legal, and personal considerations. These complexities include:

Asset Assessment: Accurately assessing the value of your assets is fundamental to estate planning. This involves not only your tangible assets such as real estate, investments, and personal belongings but also intangible assets like intellectual property, digital assets, and future income streams.

Tax Implications: Estate taxation laws can be intricate and constantly evolving. Professionals can help you navigate the complex tax landscape, ensuring that your assets are distributed efficiently and with minimal tax liabilities.

Beneficiary Designations: Deciding who should inherit your assets is a delicate matter. Professional guidance can help you make informed decisions based on factors like family dynamics, financial needs, and your personal wishes.

Guardianship and Care: If you have minor children or dependents with special needs, estate planning involves appointing guardians and setting up trusts to provide for their well-being.

Healthcare Directives: Estate planning includes documents like living wills and healthcare proxies, which dictate your medical preferences in case you become incapacitated.

Legal Professionals: The Architects of Your Estate Plan

One of the most crucial steps in estate planning is enlisting the services of an experienced attorney. Legal professionals bring invaluable expertise to the process, ensuring that your estate plan aligns with the law and your intentions.

Customized Solutions: An attorney can tailor your estate plan to your unique circumstances. They understand the intricacies of state-specific laws and can create a plan that optimizes asset protection, tax benefits, and the fulfillment of your wishes.

Will Drafting: Crafting a legally sound will is at the heart of estate planning. Lawyers have the expertise to create a will that clearly outlines your wishes and minimizes the risk of disputes or challenges.

Trust Formation: Trusts are powerful tools for managing and distributing assets. Legal professionals can help you establish trusts that protect your assets from probate, ensure privacy, and offer various tax benefits.

Updates and Maintenance: Estate plans should be periodically reviewed and updated to reflect changes in your life, such as marriage, divorce, the birth of children, or changes in your financial situation. Attorneys can guide you through these updates to ensure your plan remains current and effective.

Executor and Trustee Selection: Choosing the right individuals to serve as executors or trustees is crucial. Legal professionals can help you make informed decisions, considering factors like trustworthiness, financial acumen, and impartiality.

Financial Advisors: Maximizing Asset Efficiency

Estate planning is not solely about allocating your assets; it's also about preserving and maximizing their value. Financial advisors play a pivotal role in this aspect of estate planning.

Investment Strategies: Financial advisors can help you develop investment strategies that align with your long-term estate planning goals. These strategies may include tax-efficient investments, diversified portfolios, and risk management.

Retirement Planning: A substantial portion of your estate may be tied up in retirement accounts, such as 401(k)s and IRAs. Financial professionals can guide you in optimizing these accounts for the benefit of your heirs while minimizing tax consequences.

Life Insurance: Evaluating the need for life insurance and selecting appropriate policies can be complex. Financial advisors can assess your insurance needs and recommend suitable coverage to provide for your loved ones.

Income Distribution: If you wish to provide a steady income stream to beneficiaries, financial advisors can help structure your assets to achieve this goal efficiently.

Charitable Giving: Many individuals want to include charitable donations in their estate plans. Financial advisors can assist in creating charitable trusts or foundations to support causes close to your heart.

Minimizing Conflict and Ensuring Family Harmony

Conflict among heirs and beneficiaries is an unfortunate and all-too-common consequence of poorly structured estate plans. Seeking professional guidance is a proactive step in minimizing such conflicts and fostering family harmony.

Clarity in Wishes: Legal professionals can ensure that your will is clear, unambiguous, and free from loopholes that could lead to disputes. This clarity can prevent misunderstandings among heirs.

Fairness and Equity: Financial advisors can help you strike a balance between meeting the needs of different beneficiaries and treating them fairly. They can also assist in creating mechanisms for dispute resolution, such as mediation clauses in trusts.

Estate Equalization: In cases where some heirs receive more significant assets than others, professionals can help design strategies for estate equalization, ensuring that all heirs are treated equitably.

Transparent Communication: Open and honest communication about your estate plan with your family can prevent surprises and reduce the likelihood of conflicts arising after your passing. Legal professionals can guide you in having these crucial conversations.

The Importance of Regular Updates

Estate planning is not a one-time event. Life is dynamic, and circumstances change. Regularly reviewing and updating your estate plan is essential to ensure that it remains relevant and effective.

Changing Laws: Tax laws, inheritance laws, and regulations related to estate planning can evolve over time. Legal professionals stay abreast of these changes and can update your plan accordingly to maximize its benefits.

Life Events: Major life events such as marriage, divorce, births, deaths, or significant financial changes can impact your estate plan. Professionals can help you adapt to these changes seamlessly.

Asset Acquisitions: As you acquire new assets or dispose of existing ones, your estate plan should reflect these adjustments to maintain accuracy.

: Your goals and priorities may shift as you age or experience significant life changes. Financial advisors can help align your estate plan with your evolving objectives.

Conclusion

Estate planning is a multifaceted process that requires careful consideration of legal, financial, and personal factors. While it may be tempting to attempt a DIY (Do It Yourself) approach, the potential risks and consequences of inadequate planning make it clear that professional guidance is not optional but essential.

Legal professionals bring expertise in navigating the complex legal landscape, ensuring that your wishes are legally binding and your assets are distributed as intended. Financial advisors offer insights into maximizing asset efficiency, minimizing tax liabilities, and providing for your loved ones' financial security.

Moreover, seeking professional guidance is not just about paperwork and numbers; it's about fostering family harmony and reducing the risk of conflicts among heirs. A well-crafted estate plan, backed by expert advice, can provide peace of mind and security for you and your loved ones.

In the end, estate planning is an investment in your legacy, your family's future, and your own peace of mind. By enlisting the assistance of legal and financial professionals, you can ensure that your estate plan is a true reflection of your wishes and a source of stability and security for generations to come.

"A Guide to Estate Wills, Conflicts, and Resolutions" offers a comprehensive exploration of estate planning, focusing on the intricate world of wills and the potential conflicts that can arise within families during the estate distribution process. Starting with an introductory overview of the significance of estate planning and the fundamentals of creating a legally sound will, this book navigates readers through a journey that encompasses complex asset management, financial considerations, and the ever-changing dynamics of life and relationships.

From discussing the emotional and legal complexities of disinheriting heirs to explaining the critical role of executors and the intricacies of the probate process, this guide provides invaluable insights. It also delves into alternative dispute resolution methods, highlighting the importance of clear communication and professional guidance in achieving harmonious estate planning. Whether you're just beginning your estate planning journey or seeking solutions to existing conflicts, this book equips you with the knowledge and strategies necessary to navigate the complexities of wills and estates with confidence.

ABOUT THE AUTHOR

Mr. C. P. Kumar is a retired Scientist 'G' from National Institute of Hydrology, Roorkee, Uttarakhand, India. He is also a Reiki Healer and Chakra Balancing practitioner (with pendulum dowsing) and offers Emotional Freedom Technique (EFT) to help individuals with emotional issues. Mr. Kumar has authored many books on technical, spiritual, and social topics.

For further details, you may visit his webpage
https://www.angelfire.com/nh/cpkumar/virgo.html